D0821559

Also by Emmanuel Carrère

The Adversary

Class Trip

The Mustache

Gothic Romance

I Am Alive and You Are Dead

My Life as a Russian Novel

LIVES

OTHER THAN

MY OWN

LIVES

OTHER THAN

MY OWN

———

Emmanuel Carrère

TRANSLATED BY

Linda Coverdale

METROPOLITAN BOOKS

HENRY HOLT AND COMPANY

NEW YORK

Metropolitan Books
Henry Holt and Company, LLC
Publishers since 1866
175 Fifth Avenue
New York, New York 10010
www.henryholt.com

Originally published in France in 2009 under the title *D'autres vies que la
mienne* by P.O.L. Editeur, Paris

Library of Congress Cataloging-in-Publication Data

Carrère, Emmanuel, 1957–
[D'autres vies que la mienne. English]
Lives other than my own / Emmanuel Carrère ; translated by Linda
Coverdale.—1st ed.
   p.   cm.
ISBN 978-0-8050-9261-5 (hardcover)
I. Coverdale, Linda.   II. Title.
PQ2663.A7678D3813   2011
843'.914—dc22   2011001152

First U.S. Edition 2011

Designed by Meryl Sussman Levavi

Printed in the United States of America

1   3   5   7   9   10   8   6   4   2

LIVES

OTHER THAN

MY OWN

1

The night before the wave, I remember that Hélène and I talked about separating. It wouldn't be complicated; we didn't live together, hadn't had a child, and were even able to see ourselves remaining friends, and yet, it was sad. It was Christmas 2004. Here we were in our bungalow at the Hotel Eva Lanka, and we couldn't help remembering a different night, just after we'd met, a night we'd spent marveling that we had found each other and would never part, and would grow old together, happy for the rest of our lives. We even talked about having a child, a little girl. We did have that little girl in the end, and we still trust that we'll live out our days together. We like to think we always knew that everything would work out. But after the dazzling confidence of love at first sight came a complex, chaotic year, and what had at first seemed so certain to us (and still seems so now) no longer appeared at all certain or even desirable on that Christmas in 2004. On the contrary, we were convinced that this vacation would be our last together and that, for all our good intentions, the trip had been a mistake. Lying side by side, we couldn't bring ourselves to mention that first night and the promising future we had longed for so fervently yet seemed somehow to have lost. We were simply watching ourselves draw apart, without hostility, but with regret. It was too bad. For the umpteenth time I spoke of my inability to love, all the more remarkable in that Hélène is truly worthy of love. While I was telling myself that I would have to grow old alone, Hélène had something else to worry about: just before our departure, her sister Juliette had been hospitalized with a pulmonary embolism, and Hélène was afraid Juliette might be seriously ill or even dying. Although I insisted such fears were irrational, Hélène could not shake them off, and I resented how she had let herself become absorbed in something that excluded me. She went out on the terrace to smoke a cigarette. I waited for her, lying on the bed and thinking, If she comes back soon, if we make love, then perhaps we won't separate, perhaps we will grow old together after all. But she did not come back. She remained alone on the terrace watching the sky gradually grow lighter, listening to the birds begin to sing, and I fell asleep on my side of the bed, sad, lonely, convinced that my life could only get worse and worse.

Hélène and her son, I and mine: all four of us had signed up for a scuba lesson at the dive club in the neighboring village. Since the last session, however, my Jean-Baptiste had developed an earache and didn't want to go anymore. Tired from our almost sleepless night, Hélène and I decided to cancel the lesson. Rodrigue, the only one who'd really wanted to go diving, was disappointed. You can always go swimming in the pool, Hélène told him. Well, he'd had it up to here with swimming in the pool. He would have at least liked for someone to accompany him down to the beach below the hotel, where he wasn't allowed to go alone because of the dangerous currents, but no one wanted to go with him, neither his mother nor I, nor Jean-Baptiste, who preferred to read in the boys' bungalow. Jean-Baptiste was thirteen at the time. I had more or less forced this exotic vacation on him, a holiday with a woman he hardly knew and a boy much younger than he was, and he'd been bored from the moment we arrived, which he made clear to us by staying off on his own. Whenever I asked him irritably whether he wasn't happy to be here in Sri Lanka, he replied grudgingly that yes, yes, he was happy, but it was too hot and actually he was happiest in the bungalow, reading or playing his Game Boy. In short, he was a typical adolescent, while I was a typical father of an adolescent, catching myself telling him the same exasperating things my own parents had said to me when I was his age: You ought to go out, look around . . . What's the point of bringing you all this way? . . . Like talking to a wall. So Jean-Baptiste retreated into his lair while Rodrigue, left on his own, began bothering Hélène, who was trying to nap on a deck chair by the huge saltwater pool, where an elderly but incredibly athletic German woman who resembled Leni Riefenstahl swam every morning for two hours. As for me, still feeling sorry for myself over my inability to love, I went to hang out with the Ayurvedics, as we called the group of Swiss German guests who were staying in some nearby bungalows. They had come to the resort to follow a program of yoga and traditional Indian massage. They weren't meeting in plenary session with their master, so I performed a few asanas with them. Then I wandered back to the pool, where the last breakfast dishes had been cleared and tables were being set for lunch. Soon the tedious question would arise: What should we do that afternoon? In the three days since our arrival we had already visited the forest temple, fed the little monkeys, and seen the reclining Buddhas. So unless we undertook more ambitious cultural excursions, which none of us found tempting, we had exhausted the attractions in our immediate vicinity. Some tourists can spend days in a fishing village rhapsodizing over everything the locals do—going to market, mending nets, social rituals of all kinds—and I reproached myself for not being like that, for not having passed on to my sons the generous curiosity, the acuity of observation I admire in people like Nicolas Bouvier, the Swiss traveler and writer. I'd brought along *The Scorpion-Fish*, Bouvier's account of a year he spent in Galle, a large fortified town about thirty kilometers to the east of us along the southern coast of the island. Unlike his most famous book, *The Way of the World*, a tale of celebration and wonder, *The Scorpion-Fish* describes collapse, loss, and a descent into the abyss. It presents Sri Lanka as a form of enchantment, but in the perilous sense of the word, not some guidebook come-on for newlyweds and hip backpackers. Bouvier almost lost his mind there, and our visit, whether considered as a honeymoon or a rite of passage for a future blended family, was a failure. And a feeble failure at that, with no bang, only a whimper. I was growing anxious to go home. Crossing the trellised lobby invaded by bougainvilleas, I ran into a frustrated hotel guest who couldn't send a fax because the power was out. At the reception desk he'd heard there'd been an accident, some problem in the village, but he hadn't understood exactly what was wrong and just hoped the power would come back on soon, because his fax was very important. I rejoined Hélène, who was awake now and told me something strange was happening.

* * *

The next scene: a small gathering of guests and staff on a terrace at the end of the hotel grounds, looking out over the ocean. Curiously enough, nothing seems amiss at first. Everything appears normal. Then you start to notice how strange things really are. The water seems so far away . . . Normally, there are about twenty yards of beach between the ocean's edge and the foot of the cliff. Now, however, the sand stretches off into the distance: flat, gray, glistening in the hazy sunshine, like Mont-Saint-Michel at low tide. Then you realize that the sand is littered with objects, but you can't tell what size they are. That piece of twisted wood, is it a broken branch or a whole tree? A really big tree? That crumpled boat, perhaps that's something a bit bigger, maybe an honest-to-god trawler, shattered and tossed aside like a nutshell? There is no sound; no breath of air rustles the fronds of the coconut palms. I don't remember the first words spoken in the group we'd joined, but at one point someone murmured in English, *Two hundred children died in the village school.*

Built on the cliff overlooking the ocean, the hotel seems swathed in the exuberant vegetation of its grounds. To reach the coastal road, guests go through a guarded gate and down a concrete ramp, at the foot of which some tuk-tuks are usually waiting. Tuk-tuks are auto rickshaws, canvas-roofed motorbikes that seat two passengers, three if they squeeze together, on short trips of up to ten kilometers; for anything more, a taxi is best. There are no tuk-tuks today. Hélène and I have come down to the road to find out what's going on. Whatever it is seems serious, but except for the man who mentioned the two hundred dead children (and was immediately contradicted by someone claiming the children couldn't have been in school because it was Poya, the Buddhist celebration of the full moon), no one at the hotel knows anything

more than we do. No tuk-tuks; no passersby, either. Ordinarily
there's a constant stream: women walking in twos or threes with
their packages, schoolchildren in impeccably ironed white shirts,
everyone smiling and eager to chat. Aside from the lack of people, nothing seems different about the road, as long as we walk
beside the hill shielding us from the ocean. The moment we pass
the hill and reach the plain, we discover that to one side everything is normal—trees, flowers, low walls, small shops—while
on the other it's sheer devastation, a mire of blackish mud like a
lava flow. After walking a few more minutes toward the village,
we see a tall blond man in a torn shirt and shorts coming toward
us, haggard, covered in mud and blood. He is Dutch: strangely,
that is the first thing he tells us. The second thing is that his wife
has been injured. Some villagers have taken her in and he's seeking help, which he hopes to find at our hotel. There was an
immense wave, he says, that poured in and then receded, washing
away people and houses. He appears to be in shock, more stupefied than relieved at still being alive. Hélène offers to go with him
to the hotel, where the phone may be working again, and perhaps
there'll be a doctor among the guests. Curious, I decide to walk
on a little, and I say I'll rejoin them soon. Three kilometers along,
anguish and confusion reign at the entrance to the village. Clus-
ters of people form and dissolve as vans and pickups maneuver
through the throng; I hear cries, moans. I head down the street
that leads to the beach, but a policeman stops me. When I ask him
what has happened, he replies in English. *The sea, the water, big
water.* Is it true that people have died? *Yes, many people dead, very
dangerous. You stay in hotel? Which hotel? Eva Lanka? Good, good,
Eva Lanka, go back there, it is safe. Here, very dangerous.* Although
the danger seems over, I obey anyway.

* * *

Hélène is furious with me because I went off and left her saddled with the boys when she should have been the one to go looking for news: it's her job. While I was gone, she was contacted by LCI, the French news network for which she works as a writer and anchor. It's past midnight in Europe, which explains why the other hotel guests have not yet been phoned by panic-stricken friends and family, but the journalists on call at the major news agencies already know that Southeast Asia has been hit by something enormous, way beyond the local flooding I had initially imagined. Knowing that Hélène is vacationing here, her network had been hoping for some on-the-spot reporting and she'd had almost nothing to tell them. And I—what do I have to report? What did I see in the village of Tangalla? Not much, I admit. Hélène shrugs. I retreat to our bungalow. I'd felt energized, getting back to the hotel, because our flagging vacation had received an extraordinary jolt, but now I'm irritated by our tiff and my sense of not having risen to the occasion. Disappointed in myself, I seek refuge in *The Scorpion-Fish* and am struck by this sentence, sandwiched between two descriptions of insects: "I would have liked, this morning, a stranger's hand to close my eyes; I was alone, so I closed them myself."

In great distress, Jean-Baptiste comes to get me in the bungalow. The French couple whom we met two days earlier has just arrived at the hotel. Their daughter is dead. My son needs me to help him deal with this. Walking with him on the path to the main building, I remember when we first met the family, in one of the straw-hut restaurants on the beach I was heading to when the policeman stopped me. They'd been at a neighboring table. The husband in his early thirties, the wife her late twenties. Both good-looking, cheerful, friendly, clearly much in love and completely enamored with their four-year-old daughter, who had wandered over to play with Rodrigue, which is why we'd struck up a conversation. Unlike us, they knew the country well and were staying not at the hotel but in a little beach house the young woman's father rented by the year, about two hundred yards from the restaurant. They were the sort of people you're glad to meet when you're abroad, and we'd said good night with every intention of getting together again. Nothing official; we'd certainly be running into one another in the village and at the beach.

Hélène is in the bar talking to the couple and an older man with curly gray hair and birdlike features. That other evening, we hadn't even exchanged names, so Hélène makes the introductions. Jérôme. Delphine. Philippe. Philippe is Delphine's father, the renter of the beach house. And the little girl who died was Juliette. Hélène repeats the name in a neutral voice; Jérôme nods in confirmation. His face and Delphine's remain expressionless. I ask, Are you sure? Jérôme replies that yes, they've just come from identifying the body at the village hospital. Delphine stares straight ahead; I'm not sure she sees us. We seven—four of us, three of them—are sitting in teak armchairs and on banquettes with colorful cushions, around a low table set with fruit juices and tea. When a waiter arrives to take care of us, Jean-Baptiste and I automatically order something, and then silence falls again. It lasts until Philippe suddenly begins to speak. To no one in particular. His voice is piercing, halting, like a machine breaking down. In the hours to come, he will tell his story several times, almost word for word.

This morning, right after breakfast, Jérôme and Delphine had left for the market while Philippe stayed home to watch Juliette and

Osandi, the daughter of the beach house owner. Sitting in his wicker armchair on the bungalow terrace, Philippe read the local paper, glancing up now and then to keep an eye on the two little girls playing at the water's edge. They were jumping and laughing in the wavelets. Juliette was speaking French, and Osandi Sinhala, but they understood each other just fine. Crows were cawing, squabbling over the breakfast crumbs. All was calm; the day promised to be beautiful, and Philippe thought he might go fishing that afternoon with Jérôme. At some point, he realized that the crows had vanished and that he no longer heard any birds singing. That's when the wave hit. A moment earlier the sea was smooth; an instant later it was a wall as high as a skyscraper and it was falling on them. He thought in a flash that he was going to die but would not have time to suffer. He was submerged, swept away, and tossed around for what seemed an eternity in the immense belly of the wave before he surfaced on his back. He passed like a surfer over houses, over trees, over the road. Then the wave reversed itself, rushed in the opposite direction, sweeping him seaward. He saw he was going to smash into some collapsed walls straight ahead and tried instinctively to cling to a coconut palm but lost his grip, grabbed another, and would have lost his hold again if something hard, a section of fence, hadn't trapped him, pinning him against the palm. Furniture, animals, people, wooden beams, chunks of concrete raced past; he closed his eyes, expecting to be crushed by some huge hunk of debris, and he kept them closed until the monstrous roaring of the current died down, allowing him to hear other sounds, the cries of wounded men and women. Then he understood that the world had not come to an end, that he was alive, and that now the real nightmare was beginning.

He opened his eyes. He slid down the palm trunk to the surface of the water, which was completely black, opaque. There was

still some current, but it could be resisted. A woman's body
floated past, arms crossed, head under water. In the wreckage,
survivors were calling to one another, while the injured moaned
aloud. Philippe hesitated. Should he go toward the beach or the
village? Juliette and Osandi were dead, of that he was certain.
And he had to find Jérôme and Delphine to tell them. That was
now his task in life. Philippe was in a bathing suit, up to his chest
in the water, bleeding, but unable to determine exactly where
he'd been hurt. He would rather have simply waited there for
help, but he forced himself to set out. Beneath his bare feet the
ground was uneven, soft, unstable, carpeted with a slurry of
things he couldn't see, some of which had sharp edges, so he was
desperately afraid he would be cut again. Feeling his way carefully with each step, he made slow progress. A hundred yards
from his house, he recognized nothing: not one wall left whole,
not a single tree. A few times he saw a familiar face, neighbors
floundering like him, black with mud, red with blood, eyes wide
with horror, searching like him for those they loved. The sucking
noise of the retreating waters had almost completely given way to
increasingly loud screams, wails, groans. Philippe finally reached
the road and, a little higher up, the place where the wave had
stopped. It was uncanny, that boundary marked so distinctly.
Over here, chaos; over there, the everyday world, absolutely
intact: small houses of pink or pale green brick, paths of reddish
laterite, market stalls, people bustling about, wearing clothes,
alive, and only now beginning to grasp—without knowing exactly
what it was—that something horrendous had occurred. The zom-
bies who, like Philippe, were trying to get their footing back in
the land of the living could only stammer the word *wave*, and this
word spread through the village just as the word *plane* must have
done in Manhattan on September 11. Spasms of panic carried
people both toward the ocean, to see what had happened and

to help those needing rescue, and as far away from the water as possible, in case the wave came back. Amid the shouting and confusion, Philippe made his way along the main street to the market, where the morning crowds of shoppers would have been at their height, and as he was steeling himself for a prolonged and agonizing search, he saw Delphine and Jérôme at the foot of the clock tower. They'd just heard such garbled news of the disaster that Jérôme was wondering if a crazed gunman had opened fire somewhere in Tangalla. Philippe went toward them, knowing that they were living their last moments of happiness. The couple spotted him approaching; then he stood before them, smeared with mud and blood, his face contorted with emotion, and at this point in his story Philippe stops. He can't go on. His mouth hangs open, but he can't repeat the three words he must have said to them.

Delphine screamed; Jérôme didn't. He took Delphine in his arms and hugged her as tightly as he could while she screamed and screamed, and from then on he had only one objective: *I can no longer do anything for my daughter, so I will save my wife.* I wasn't there to see what happened, I'm describing the scene according to what Philippe said, but I did witness what followed and I saw Jérôme's program at work. He did not waste time hoping in vain. Philippe was not only his father-in-law but a friend in whom he had complete confidence, so he understood immediately that no matter what shock and disorientation Philippe had suffered, if he'd said those three words, they were true. Delphine, however, wanted to believe her father was mistaken. He was himself a survivor, so perhaps Juliette was as well. Philippe shook his head: impossible. Juliette and Osandi had been at the water's very edge, they'd never had a chance. No chance at all. They found her at

the hospital, among the dozens—no, already the hundreds of
corpses the ocean had given back and that now lay, for lack of
room, right on the floor. Osandi and her father lay there, too.

As the afternoon wears on, the hotel becomes a kind of Raft of
the Medusa. Tourists who've survived the tidal wave have been
told that they will be safe here, and they stumble in almost naked,
often injured, in total shock. Rumor has it that a second wave may
be coming. The locals have sought refuge on the other side of the
coastal road, as far from the ocean as they can get, while the foreigners seek safety in elevation, meaning with us. Philippe has
made the first of a series of wrenching calls to Isabelle on his cell
phone, and although telephone lines are down, as the day goes
on cell phones begin ringing all around us, as terrified family
and friends who have just heard the news start calling. Their
loved ones reassure them quickly, succinctly, to save their phone
batteries. That evening the hotel management runs a generator
for a few hours so people can recharge them and follow developments on television. At one end of the bar is a giant screen
that usually shows soccer matches, since the hotel proprietors
are Italian, as are many of the guests. Everyone—guests, staff,
survivors—gathers to watch CNN and we discover the scale of
the catastrophe. Images come in from Sumatra, Thailand, the
Maldives; all Southeast Asia and the Indian Ocean have been
affected. We begin to see short film loops shot by amateurs
showing the wave approaching in the distance, the torrents of
mud pouring into houses, sweeping everything away. Now we all
talk about the tsunami as if we'd always known what that word
meant.

* * *

We have dinner with Delphine, Jérôme, and Philippe; we sit with them again at breakfast the next morning, then at lunch, then again at dinner, and until our return to Paris we are always together. They don't behave like beaten people to whom nothing matters and who cannot cope. They want to go home with Juliette's body, and from that first evening on, the terrifying void of her absence is kept at bay by practical problems. Jérôme tackles them with everything he's got: it's his way of remaining alive, of keeping Delphine alive, and Hélène helps him by trying to contact their insurance company on her cell phone to organize their departure and the shipment of the body. It isn't easy, obviously, what with the distance, the time difference, and the overloaded circuits. She's often put on hold, spending precious minutes of battery life listening to soothing music and recorded messages, then when she finally speaks to an actual person, she's transferred to another line where the music starts up again—or she's cut off. These ordinary annoyances, simply irritating in everyday life, become in this emergency both monstrous yet vital, because they define tasks to be accomplished, give form to the passage of time. There is something to do: Jérôme is doing it, Hélène is helping him, it's as simple as that. While this is going on, Jérôme keeps an eye on Delphine. Delphine stares into space. She doesn't cry, doesn't scream. Although she eats very little, that's better than nothing. Her hand shakes but she can bring a forkful of curried rice to her lips. Put it in her mouth. Chew it. Load more rice on the fork. Eat another mouthful. I look at Hélène and feel clumsy, helpless, useless. I almost resent her for being so caught up in the task at hand that she's paying no attention to me. It's as if I no longer exist.

Later, we're lying on the bed, side by side. My fingertips caress hers, which don't respond. I'd like to take her in my arms but I know that isn't possible. I know what she's thinking; it's impossible to think of anything else. A few dozen yards from us, in another bungalow, Jérôme and Delphine must be lying down as well, wide awake. Has he taken her in his arms, or is that impossible for them as well? It's the first night. The night of the day their daughter died. This morning she was alive, she woke up, she came to play in their bed, she called them Mama and Papa, she was laughing, she was warm, she was the loveliest and warmest and sweetest thing on earth, and now she's dead. She will always be dead.

Since the beginning of our stay, I'd been saying that I didn't like the Hotel Eva Lanka and suggesting that we move into one of the little beach guesthouses, which weren't nearly as comfortable as our bungalows but reminded me of my backpacking trips twenty-five or thirty years ago. I wasn't really serious; in my descriptions of those marvelous lodgings, I gleefully emphasized the lack of electricity, the mosquito nets full of holes, the poisonous spiders that dropped onto your head. Hélène and the children would shriek, making fun of my old hippie nostalgia, and the whole thing had become a comic routine. The beach guesthouses were swept away by the wave, along with most of their guests. I think, We might have been among them. Jean-Baptiste might have gone down to the beach with Rodrigue. We might have, as planned, gone out on a boat with the scuba diving instructor. And Delphine and Jérôme—they must be thinking, We could have taken Juliette to the market. If we had, she would have come bouncing into our bed tomorrow morning. The world around us would be in mourning but we would hug our little girl and say, Thank God, she's here, that's all that matters.

2

___

On the morning of the second day, Jérôme says, I'm going to check on Juliette. As if he wants to make sure she's being well cared for. Go ahead, says Delphine. Jérôme leaves with Philippe. Hélène lends a bathing suit to Delphine, who does the breast-stroke in the hotel pool for a long time, slowly, staring straight ahead. There are now three or four families of tourist "survivors" around the pool, but they have lost only their belongings and don't dare complain much in front of Delphine. The Swiss Germans calmly stick to their Ayurvedic schedule as if nothing has happened. Philippe and Jérôme return at noon, looking haggard: Juliette is no longer in the Tangalla hospital. She's been moved— perhaps to Matara, or maybe Colombo. There are too many bodies; some are being burned, others have been transferred to hospitals less overwhelmed, and rumors of epidemics are starting to circulate. All Jérôme could obtain was a scrap of paper with a few scribbled words a hotel employee now translates for him with mortified sympathy. It's a kind of receipt, stating simply, "Little white girl, blond, in a red dress."

Hélène and I now go to Tangalla. The tuk-tuk driver chatters away: *Many people dead*, but his wife and children, thank God, are safe. When we approach the hospital, we're hit by the foul odor. Even if you've never breathed it before, you know what it is. *Dead bodies, many dead bodies*, says the driver, bringing a hand-kerchief to his nose while gesturing for us to do the same. In the courtyard, only a few men wear hospital uniforms; the rest must be volunteers in street clothes. They're all carrying stretchers, pil-ing bodies into the back of a covered truck, one on top of another. Once filled, the trucks leave; others arrive. We enter a large room that seems more like a fish market than a hospital lobby. The con-crete floor is damp and slippery, hosed down occasionally to sug-gest a hint of coolness. Bodies lie in rows; I count about forty of them. They've been here since yesterday, many of them swollen from their time in the water. No foreigners; perhaps they were given priority evacuation, like Juliette. Their skin isn't really dark, it's gray. I've never seen a dead person before; it feels strange to have been spared this until the age of forty-seven. Pressing a bit of cloth to our noses, we check other rooms, go upstairs. It's hard to tell visitors from staff. No one stops us, no doors are closed, and there are corpses everywhere, bloated and grayish. I remem-ber the rumors about epidemics, and the Dutchman at the hotel declaring that if all the bodies weren't burned right away, we'd have a health catastrophe for sure: the cadavers would poison the wells and rats would spread cholera through all the villages. I'm afraid even to breathe, as if the fearsome odor were infectious. I wonder what we're doing here. Looking. Just looking. Hélène is the only journalist in this area. She already dictated an article yesterday evening and another one this morning, and she's brought her camera but hasn't the heart to take it out. She questions a visibly exhausted doctor in English, but we can't really understand his replies. Back in the courtyard, the truck we'd seen being loaded with corpses has left. Outside the gate, beside the road, there is a patch of dry, sharp-edged grass shaded by an immense banyan tree, at the foot of which wait a dozen people: whites, in torn clothing and covered with small wounds they haven't bothered to treat. When we go over to them, they gather around us. They've all lost someone—wife, husband, child, friend—but unlike Delphine and Jérôme, they haven't seen their bodies and will not give up hope. Ruth, a redhead of about twenty-five from Scotland, is the first to speak. She was in a beach bungalow with Tom: they'd just gotten married and were on their honeymoon. When the wave struck they were within ten yards of each other, but Tom was swept away while she survived by clinging to a tree the same way Philippe did, and she's been looking for Tom ever since. She's searched everywhere—on the beach, among the ruins, in the village, at the police station—and having learned that all bodies eventually get sent to the hospital, she has come here, and here she stays. She's looked all through the hospital several times; she watches every truck deliver its new corpses and load up those bound for cremation. She hasn't eaten or slept. The hospital staff have told her to go rest, promising to let her know of any news, but she won't leave, she wants to stay with her companions, who stay for the same reasons. They know that any news can only be bad. But they want to be here when their loved ones' bodies come off the truck. She's been waiting since yesterday evening, so Ruth knows how things work here: she confirms that any whites brought in are quickly moved about fifteen kilometers to the east

along the southern coast, to Matara, where there is more space
and, apparently, a refrigerated cold room. The villagers are supposed to claim their dead here, but many families, especially
fishermen who lived near the water, were wiped out, leaving no
one to come for those bodies, which are unceremoniously sent to
be burned. All this happens in a chaotic, slapdash manner. Since
the hospital has no electricity or phone service and the local roads
are in bad shape, there's little hope of receiving help from the
outside anytime soon. And what would that even mean, "outside," when the whole island has been affected? No one has
escaped; all are dealing with their dead. That's what Ruth says,
yet she sees that Hélène and I have escaped. We are still together,
our clothes are clean, and we aren't searching for anyone in particular. After our visit to hell, we will return to our hotel, where
lunch will be served to us. We will swim in the pool, we'll kiss
our children and think, We came so close . . . A guilty conscience
is pointless, I know, but mine torments me anyway and I'm ready
to move on, whereas Hélène completely ignores her feelings and
devotes all her energy to doing what she can, because even if it's
something paltry, she must still do it. She's attentive, careful, asks
questions, thinks of everything that can be useful. She has
brought all our cash with her and distributes it among Ruth and
her companions. She writes down everyone's name, along with
the name and a brief description of each missing person. Tomorrow she will try to get to Matara and will look for them there. She
notes the phone numbers of everyone's families in Europe and
America, so she can call them later to say, I saw Ruth, she's alive;
I saw Peter, he's alive. She offers to take whoever wants to come
with us back to the hotel, since only one or two people need to
keep watch; the others could eat, wash, receive first aid, sleep a
little, phone home, then return to relieve the others. But no one
wants to come with us.

* * *

Among those keeping vigil that day across from the hospital, Ruth is the one I remember best because we spoke chiefly to her and because we saw her again later, but there was also an overweight middle-aged Englishwoman with short hair who had lost her girl-friend. I imagined the two of them getting on in years, living in a lovingly tended house in an English town, taking part in its social life, going on a yearly trip to some distant country, putting together their photo albums . . . All that shattered. The survivor's return; the empty house. Each woman's mug with her name on it, one of them forever forlorn. And this heavy woman, sitting slumped at the kitchen table with her head in her hands, weeping, telling her-self that she's all alone now and will be until she dies. In the months that followed our return to France, Hélène was obsessed with the idea of contacting the people in the group to learn what had happened to them and to see if anyone had been graced by a miracle. But no matter how hard she looked through our luggage for her list of survivors, she couldn't find it, and we resigned our-selves to never learning more about them. The image I have today of the half hour we spent under the banyan is something from a horror film. There we are, neat and clean, untouched, while around us cluster the lepers, poisoned by radiation, shipwrecked souls reduced to a savage state. Only yesterday evening they were like us and we like them, but something happened to them and not us, so now we belong to two separate branches of humanity.

That evening, Philippe tells us how his love affair with Sri Lanka first began over twenty years ago. He was a computer specialist in a Parisian suburb dreaming of distant lands when he became friends with a Sri Lankan colleague, who later invited the whole family home to his island: Philippe, his then wife, and little Delphine. It was their first big trip together and they fell in love with everything about the island: the bustling cities, cool mountain retreats, languid seaside villages, terraced rice fields, chirping geckos, roofs of fluted tiles, forest temples, the dazzlingly bright smiles and sunrises, and eating curried rice with their fingers. Philippe had thought, This is real life, this is where I'd like to live one day. That day took some time to arrive, however. The Sri Lankan colleague moved to Australia, and after a few letters contact was lost, the connection to the enchanting island broken. But Philippe had had enough of being a suburban midlevel manager. He had a passionate interest in wine and decided to explore it. Back then a computer specialist could easily get well-paid work wherever he wanted, so he moved to a village near Saint-Émilion and quickly found clients—purchase centers, distributors, major wineries—for whom he modernized and supervised management systems. In a region where people had a reputation for being standoffish to newcomers, his wife opened a shop that did surprisingly well. The family lived in the country from then on, in a pretty house surrounded by grapevines, earning a good living doing things they enjoyed. Their new lifestyle was a success. Later Philippe met Isabelle, and was amicably divorced from his wife. Delphine grew up, a smart and delightful girl who first saw Jérôme when she was just shy of fifteen and knew even then he would be the man of her life. He was twenty-one, strong and handsome, the heir to a long line of wealthy wine merchants. Differences in fortune are no small matter in that milieu, but in time a teenager's dream became a serious engagement. Displaying quiet determination, Jérôme stood up to his family: he loved Delphine, he had chosen Delphine, and no one was going to make him change his mind. Since Philippe worshipped his daughter, there was reason to fear no suitor would please him, but once again it was love at first sight: a deep bond of affection united father- and son-in-law. Despite the twenty-year difference in their ages, they shared the same tastes: great Bordeaux, the Rolling Stones, fishing, and, to cap it all, Delphine. The two men were soon as thick as thieves. When the newlyweds found a house in a village about ten kilometers from the one where Philippe and Isabelle lived, the two couples became inseparable. The four of them often had dinner at one house or the other, where Philippe and Jérôme would take turns producing bottles for blind tastings, and after talking legs, nose, body, mouthfeel, they'd light up an after-dinner joint of homegrown weed smoked to the strains of *Angie* or *Satisfaction*. They all loved one another and were happy. Out under his pergola, Philippe would ramble on about Sri Lanka, and although it had been a good eight years since their first trip, he and Delphine still remembered the island with pleasure. One autumn evening, right after the grape harvest, they were dining outside; they'd drunk a Château-Magdelaine 1967 (the year Jérôme was born) and were talking about vacationing there, all four of them, when Isabelle had an idea: How about if the boys went over first to do some reconnoitering?

For "the boys," their five weeks of scouting in Sri Lanka became a magical memory. Backpacking with a travel guide for the hip and frugal, they traipsed around by tuk-tuk, train, and bus, lucking into village festivals and chance encounters, living on the spur of the moment. Philippe was proud to show his island to Jérôme and then a little irritated, but in the end even prouder, to see that after a few days his son-in-law was managing better than he was himself. With his even temper and gentle sense of irony, Jérôme seems to me the ideal travel companion: letting things happen, never in a hurry, treating setbacks as opportunities, seeing every stranger as a possible friend. More excitable, more talkative, Philippe whirled around his tranquil broad-shouldered companion the way the frantic half of a comic duo plays up to the straight man in a buddy comedy. It must have amused them both no end, when chatting with other travelers on guesthouse verandas, to surprise everyone by announcing they were father- and son-in-law.

They headed south. They took their sweet time traveling the coastal road from Colombo to Tangalla, a stretch we covered by taxi in half a day, and the more the road twisted and turned as it left the capital behind, the more their lives seemed to stretch out between the surf and the coconut palms into something timeless, Edenic. The last real city on this coast is Galle, the Portuguese fortress where Nicolas Bouvier had ended up alone forty years earlier to live a long season in hell in the company of termites and ghosts. Having no particular affinity for hell, Philippe and Jérôme went on their way whistling. After Galle, there are only a few little fishing towns: Weligama, Matara, Tangalla, and, just beyond that, a little spot called Medaketiya, a handful of houses in green or pink brick corroded by the salt spray and a jungle of coconut palms, banana plants, and mango trees that drop their fruit right onto your plate. On the white sand beach: outrigger canoes in bright colors, nets, shacks. No hotel, but a few of the shacks serve as guesthouses and the guy who owns them is called MH. Well, he actually has one of those Sri Lankan names with at least twelve syllables, without which a man has no substance on this earth, but to make life easier for foreigners he calls himself MH, pronounced as in English: Em Aitch. Medaketiya and MH's guesthouses were the dream of every beach bum in the world. It was *the* beach, the end of the road, the place where you finally settle in. Smiling folks, easygoing, who won't cheat you. Not many tourists, and those few are like you: individualists, quiet, jealously guarding this secret spot. Philippe and Jérôme spent three days there swimming, dining in the evening on the fish they'd caught that morning, drinking beer, and smoking joints while congratulating each other on the success of their scouting expedition: paradise on earth did exist, they'd found it, now all they had to do was bring along their wives.

When they announced to MH at the end of their stay that they would soon be back, MH responded politely with the Sri Lankan equivalent of *inshallah*, but all four of them did show up the following year, and the next year, and the year after that. Their lives slowly organized themselves around two poles, Saint-Émilion and Medaketiya. While Philippe managed to spend three or four months in Medaketiya, the rest of the family was more tied down and came only on vacation. (Isabelle, for example, who spent much of her time at her boutique in Arcachon, was back home in France when the tsunami hit on that Boxing Day in 2004.) In Medaketiya, Philippe always stayed with MH, who gradually became a close friend and even visited them all once in the Gironde. The trip was not a huge success. Out of his own setting, MH was ill at ease and did not become a convert to *les grands crus borde-lais*. So it goes.

Philippe eventually left the guesthouse to take up quarters in a bungalow that he rented from MH by the year and that he and Isabelle fixed up as they pleased, making it a real home. They had a house in Medaketiya, friends in Medaketiya. Everyone knew them there and loved them. Juliette was born and they brought the baby with them to Medaketiya. Along with his grown sons, MH also had a little girl named Osandi. Three years older than Juliette, Osandi quickly learned how to take care of her: she was her big sister.

What Philippe loved best was to go out there a month before the others and live alone in Medaketiya, knowing they would all be joining him soon. He enjoyed both the solitude and the happi-ness of having a family: a wife who suited him perfectly and vice versa, a daughter so marvelous that she'd managed to marry a man who'd become her father's best friend, and a granddaughter who was the image of her mother at that age. Enough said. Really, it was a good life. Philippe had known when to take risks—the move to Saint-Émilion, a new profession, his divorce—but had never chased pipe dreams or broken anyone's heart beyond repair, and he no longer wanted to conquer anything. He just wished to savor what he already had: contentment. He shared with Jérôme a trait rare in someone his age, a slightly sardonic way of looking at go-getters who plot and fume and stress themselves, always jockeying for position, never satisfied. Philippe and his son-in-law were men who did their work well, but once it was done and the reward received, they relaxed, enjoying the fruits of their labor instead of taking on more work to make more money. They were fortunate in that they had enough to be satisfied with their lot, but above all they had the wisdom to actually *be* satisfied, to love what they had and not crave more. They allowed themselves to live at a leisurely pace without feeling guilty, to carry on a relaxed and amusing conversation in the shade of a banyan, sipping beer. *We must cultivate our garden. Carpe diem.* To live happily, live hidden, as a French proverb says. That's not how Philippe puts it, but it's how I understand him, and as he speaks I feel far away from such wisdom, I who live in dissatisfaction, constant tension, running after dreams of glory and laying waste to my loves because I always imagine that one day, somewhere else, I'll find something better.

Philippe was thinking, I've found the place where I want to live, where I want to die. I've brought my family here and here I've found a second family, MH's. When I close my eyes in my wicker armchair, when I feel the wooden floor of the bungalow's front porch beneath my bare feet, when I hear the coconut fiber broom MH wields every morning swishing over his sandy yard with such a peaceful, familiar sound, I tell myself, You're home. In your own house. His housekeeping done, MH will come join me, calm and majestic in his scarlet sarong. We'll smoke a cigarette together. We'll exchange a few casual words, like old friends who need not speak to understand each other. I believe I've really become Sri Lankan, Philippe remarked to MH one day, and he remembers the friendly but somewhat ironic look in MH's eyes: *You think so, huh* . . . Philippe had been a trifle irritated, but he'd seen the point: he'd become a friend, yes, but he was still a foreigner. His life, no matter what he believed, was elsewhere.

Today Philippe might well think, My granddaughter died in Medaketiya, our happiness was destroyed here in a matter of seconds, and I don't ever want to hear of this place again. But that's not what he thinks. He thinks he will finally prove to his dead friend MH that his life is indeed here, among them, that he's one of them, that after sharing with them the sweetness of life he will not turn away from their misfortune, will not pick up his marbles and say, So long, maybe we'll meet again someday. He thinks about what remains of MH's family, about their destroyed homes and those of their fishermen neighbors, and he says, I want to stay by their side. To help them rebuild, begin living again. He wants to make himself useful. What else can he do with himself?

3

We don't know when we'll be able to leave. We don't know where Juliette's body was taken—to the hospital in Matara, perhaps, or to Colombo. Jérôme, Delphine, and Philippe will not leave Sri Lanka without her, and we won't leave without them. Matara is too far to go to by tuk-tuk, but the hotel manager announces at breakfast that he has arranged for Jérôme to ride with a police van heading in that direction. Hélène immediately offers to accompany him and Jérôme immediately accepts. I believe I should have offered to go, it's a job for a man, and I watch them leave with a shameful pang of jealousy. I feel like a child left home by adults who are off dealing with grown-up things, the way Jean-Baptiste and Rodrigue must have felt, left on their own for the past forty-eight hours while Hélène and I have been concerned almost exclusively with Philippe, Delphine, and Jérôme.

The boys have spent their days holed up in their bungalow rereading old comic books, joining us only for meals they eat in silence, sulking and feeling out of place. I suddenly see that it must be hard for them to be part of a cataclysmic event like this and yet be sheltered as if they were little kids. I suppose that seeing nothing can be more traumatizing than seeing corpses and that Jean-Baptiste, at least, is old enough to go to Medaketiya with me and Philippe, who is busy with his plans to help out and wants to evaluate the situation for himself. I'm a little reluctant to leave Rodrigue with Delphine, but she insists that he'll be no problem, so we set out.

The tuk-tuk gives the hospital a wide berth, but not wide enough to spare us the stench of death. When I catch a distant glimpse of the band of shipwrecked tourists milling around beneath the banyan, I feel yet again like a survivor in a zombie film, driving past a listless gathering of the living dead, who follow us with their empty eyes. The main street is eerily calm. We reach the marketplace where Philippe told Jérôme and Delphine of Juliette's death, then drive down to the beach at Medaketiya, a field of reeking black mud from which protrudes the debris left by boats, houses, fences, uprooted tree trunks, and an occasional stretch of wall, still standing. Out among the ruins, people are busy dredging, searching, recovering all manner of objects: a basin, a fishing net, a chipped plate; this is all they have left. Everyone recognizes Philippe when we appear. They come up to him a few at a time, and it's practically the same scene over and over: they hug, they weep together, and in garbled English his friends deliver their news, which is essentially a litany of the dead. Philippe has nothing to tell them; they already know about Juliette, Osandi, and MH, but he's hearing for the first time about his neighbors, and with each name they mention he lets out, like those around him, a kind of moan. He wasn't boasting when he claimed to know everyone, to have been adopted by them all. He mourns these Sri Lankan fisherfolk as if they were his relatives. He tries to explain to each survivor that though he must leave now, right away, with Delphine and Jérôme, he will return soon, after finding some money, and will stay a long time to help. It seems very important to him to tell them this, and important for them to hear it; in any case, they all hug him again. We move from one pile of wreckage to another, from survivor to survivor, embrace to embrace, until we reach MH's little property. There's nothing left of the guest-houses, and of the bungalow Philippe rented, only a few floor-boards and a shower bucket remain, along with part of a wall decorated with a brightly colored mural of coconut palms, nets, and fish. Delphine had painted it last year with Juliette. They'd both taken great pains with it; Juliette had been three, proud to be helping her mother. Philippe sits down in front of the paint-ing, surrounded by rubbish. Jean-Baptiste and I step back a little and watch him.

Would you do the same thing, in his place? Jean-Baptiste blurts out.

Would I do what?

If your four-year-old granddaughter were dead, or Gabriel and I, your sons, if we were dead, would you do stuff for the fish-ermen of Medaketiya?

I hesitate. I don't know.

Well, says Jean-Baptiste, I don't think I'd give a damn about any fishing families in Medaketiya.

After a little thought, I say that giving a damn is either proof of incredible generosity or a survival strategy, which is how I pre-fer to think of it. That just seems more human. Sometimes think-ing of yourself is what is most human. Caring about humanity in general when your child is dead? I don't believe that, but I don't think that's what Philippe and Jérôme are concerned about. I believe they're trying to survive Juliette's death. And most of all, they want to save Delphine.

Back at the hotel, I try to reach Hélène on her cell but she doesn't answer. At lunchtime, she and Jérôme are still not back; after waiting a bit, we eat without them. For the last two days, the Italians running the hotel have been beyond reproach: they are feeding and lodging everyone, showing the same consideration to paying guests and penniless refugees, and although the meals are growing skimpier for lack of supplies, the service remains as casually elegant as it was before the catastrophe. Nervous, uneasy, I check my watch. I wouldn't admit it for the world but the truth is, I see the situation this way: my wife has gone off to live an intense experience with another man. I, who two days ago found her glum and dull, now see her as the heroine of a novel or an adventure film, the brave and beautiful journalist who in the heat of action holds nothing back. In this novel or film, I am not the hero, alas; I see myself rather as the insipid husband, a cautious and caustic diplomat, perfectly suited to cocktails and garden parties at the embassy but who, when the Khmer Rouge surround the place, fails to measure up, dithers, waits for others to make decisions for him, and when his wife goes off bravely to the front lines to stare death in the face, watches her leave with someone else. I feel increasingly anxious, so to take the edge off waiting, I return to *The Scorpion-Fish.* I'm reading a chapter that describes Matara as a village of particularly redoubtable sorcerers when I come across this sentence: "If we knew how vulnerable it makes us, we'd never dare to be happy." This does not concern me, since I have never dared to be happy. I play a game of chess with Jean-Baptiste;

with Rodrigue, I collaborate on a series of fairly grotesque people drawn on paper we fold in such a way that we can't see what
the other has created. It's a game I taught him, inspired by the
Surrealists, called Exquisite Corpse, and when Rodrigue repeats
the name I tell him to lower his voice. Hearing something in my
tone, he understands immediately, glancing ruefully over at Delphine.

When I talk with her later, she tells me about her life in Saint-
Émilion. She's always loved nature, has never imagined living any-
where but in the country. And has never tried to assert herself or
be independent by working, either: she's been a stay-at-home
mother and has no hang-ups about it; she and Jérôme have divided
up the traditional tasks in a natural and even modern way. Jérôme
worked, she took care of Juliette, the house, the garden, the animals. Juliette adored the animals, especially the rabbits, which
she insisted on feeding herself. Jérôme would come home every
day for lunch and take his time, time to chat and relax with his
wife, to enjoy the meal she'd prepared, to play with their daughter. He worked, yes, but at his own pace, always available to his
wife and daughter, to his father-in-law, to their handful of friends,
and to a few close clients who were an extension of the inner circle within which flourished the family's happiness. Listening to
Delphine, I study her: blond, gracious, charming, guileless. Her
father says that she looks like the singer Vanessa Paradis—or
rather, and he insists on this small point, that Vanessa Paradis
looks like her. It's true, but even though I saw Juliette only once,
for half an hour, what I really think is that Delphine looks like
her daughter. I try to imagine their life, so peaceful and different
from my own. Delphine describes it calmly, but as if she were
sleepwalking, as if it were all in the past.

* * *

Later, Ruth arrives at the hotel. After spending forty-eight hours outside the hospital without eating or sleeping, she's incredibly weak and she has been brought here more or less by force. In front of her sits a sandwich she hasn't touched; the oldest of the Italians running the hotel comes to announce that a room has been prepared for her. He insists gently that she should go lie down, sleep a little, but she shakes her head. When she was under the banyan, she didn't want to move. Now that she's been uprooted and planted in this armchair, she doesn't want to move from there, either, and certainly not to go to bed. She thinks that if she falls asleep, Tom won't be able to come back. To make it possible for him to return, she must remain awake. She would really like to go sit on the beach right where the wave separated them, where their bungalow was, and stay there, staring at the horizon, until Tom walks alive out of the ocean. She sits up straight when she says that, as if she were meditating, and you can imagine her waiting on the beach like that for days, weeks, without eating or sleeping or speaking, breathing more and more slowly and quietly, ceasing little by little to be human, turning into a statue. Her determination is frightening; you can sense that she's quite close to passing to the other side, into catatonia, living death, and Delphine and I understand that our role is to prevent this. Which means convincing her that Tom will not return, that he drowned like the others. Two days have passed; he's almost certainly dead. Trying to help Ruth the way Jérôme is helping her, Delphine tells her own story. She tells Ruth what others have been saying in her presence, something I haven't heard her say, however, until this moment: her little girl is dead. She says the words in her schoolgirl English: *My little girl is dead.* Ruth asks only one question: Did you see her dead? Delphine has to say yes, and Ruth replies, Then it's not the same. Me, I haven't seen Tom dead. As long as I haven't seen him, I won't believe he's dead. Believing that would be like killing him.

Ruth doesn't grasp much of what's said to her, but we can get her to talk, it's a way of maintaining a connection. She is a social worker, Tom a carpenter. She refuses to believe in his death, but she says, *He was a carpenter.* The past tense is already eating into her story. She and Tom have known and loved each other since they were teenagers. Married last autumn, they left the day after their wedding to spend a year traveling around the world. They knew what they would do when they returned: have their first child—they wanted three—and begin building their house. In a village not far from Glasgow, they'd gone into debt to buy a bit of land with a tumbledown stone barn Tom intended to restore. This would probably take around two years, because Tom would be able to work on the barn only in his spare time, so meanwhile they would live in a trailer. The baby would spend its first year there, but after that they and their children would have a house, a real one, all their own, which neither Ruth nor Tom had when they were children because they'd come from uprooted rural families and had grown up feeling lost in the city, without any real attachment there. Tom and Ruth were alike, with similar stories, and to hear Ruth tell it life hadn't been easy for them. They had the same fear of drifting, of living an unwanted, unchosen life, but they had found each other and promised to stay together for better or worse, to help each other come what might. Together they were strong, they had a plan: they would build their life and not let it simply drift along. Before devoting all their energy to this plan, before tying themselves down at home through their children, work, the repayment of their loans (all responsibilities they looked forward to shouldering), they had decided to give themselves this year of freedom, to see the wide world, just the two of them. After that they'd buckle down and keep going, working hard in a Scottish village halfway between countryside and industrial suburb where it rains three days out of four. They would have had their world tour, though: backpacks, bus stations, tropical sunrises and sunsets, odd jobs at every stop to keep their savings intact (a month washing dishes in a pizzeria in Izmir, another month at a naval shipyard in southern India), and priceless images, memories that would last them a lifetime. They could even see themselves, an old couple in the house that Tom built, the house where their children would have grown up, where their grandchildren would visit, looking at the photos of that great adventure of their youth. But if Tom isn't with Ruth anymore to share them, all memories and plans have become impossible. Youth is already over for her, and without Tom she will have no more use for old age. The wave carried away her future along with her past. She'll have no house, no children. It would be futile for us to tell her that at twenty-seven her life is not over, that after a period of mourning she will meet another man with whom something else will be possible. Because if Tom is dead, all Ruth can do is die.

Listening to her I think, This woman has lost everything— but once she had everything, at least everything that matters. Love, the desire that it last, the will to make it last, and the confidence that it would. Although I have many other riches, I envy her that treasure. I have never managed, up to now, to see myself living like that with a woman. When I'm with a woman, I never truly believe I'll grow old by her side, that she'll close my eyes or I hers. I tell myself that the next one will be the right one but at the same time I suspect that, given my track record, the next one won't be any better and in the end I'll wind up alone. Before the tidal wave, Hélène and I had been close to separating. Once again, love was falling apart; I hadn't known how to take care of it. And while Ruth evokes, in a low, toneless voice, the honeymoon photos that she and Tom were so certain they would cherish in their old age, I disconnect, go off on a tangent, searching my memory for what would be *our* equivalent of those photographs.

A few months earlier, I'd made a film of my novel *The Mustache*. During preproduction and the film shoot, Hélène and I often spent the night on the main set, the apartment of the couple played by Vincent Lindon and Emmanuelle Devos. We took a secret pleasure in sleeping in the protagonists' bed, in using their bathtub, hastily putting things back in their places before the film crew arrived in the morning. The script called for an erotic scene I had envisioned as really raw. The two actors were a little worried and kept asking me how I was planning to stage the scene, and although I always replied confidently that I had something in mind, I actually hadn't the slightest idea. I'd scheduled an entire night for scene 39 and as that night drew closer, I began to worry, too. After I shared my anxiety with Hélène, she suggested one evening on the set that we rehearse the scene, to help me visualize it more clearly. So for two nights running, before a video camera on a tripod, we rehearsed, varying and enriching the scene, putting lots of heart into our work. When the time came to film the scene for the movie, the results weren't bad, but in the end they wound up on the cutting-room floor, and it became a ritual joke to announce to the cast that we would include it on the extended edition of the DVD. In reality, a much better bonus would have been the two cassettes of homemade porn stashed in my desk drawer with the innocuous label *Outtakes, rue René-Boulanger*. And what I'm thinking this afternoon, in the bar of the Hotel Eva Lanka, where Delphine and I are listening to Ruth talk about Tom and their love, is that those two cassettes could—if we stay together, if we go through life together—become our keepsake. I imagine us watching our youthful bodies on the screen, firm, vigorous, supple, while Hélène reaches with an age-spotted hand for my old dick that has served her faithfully for thirty years, and suddenly that image moves me tremendously. I tell myself that this long life together *must* happen: if I need to succeed at one thing before I die, it's this.

Hélène and Jérôme have the intensely bright eyes of those who have been baptized by fire. Jérôme tells Delphine only that Juliette has been moved from Matara to Colombo and that he'll arrange for them all to go home as soon as possible. I'd like to hustle Hélène off to our bungalow so she can rest and fill me in, but she puts me off until later. She wants to stay with Ruth, whom she hugged when she came in as if she'd known her for ages. Hélène is exhausted, positively glowing with fatigue. We're all gathered around Ruth, united in the idea that there may still be some way to help her, save her, to tear her from the void into which she stares, motionless. Again, it's Hélène who steps up, asking if she has phoned her family in Scotland. Ruth shakes her head: What's the use? Hélène insists that she call: the same torment she feels about Tom's uncertain fate must be torturing her parents, whom she has no right to leave in the dark. Ruth doesn't want to report that Tom is dead and tries to wriggle out of calling, but Hélène assures her that she need only say that she herself is alive. You don't even have to talk, I'll do it if you want, just give me their phone number. After a moment's hesitation, without looking at Hélène, Ruth slowly recites the number. As Hélène taps it into her cell, I think about the time difference and imagine how the ringing will echo through a brick cottage in a Glasgow suburb in the middle of the night without startling anyone awake, because Ruth's parents probably haven't slept for three days. Hélène hands the phone to Ruth. They must have picked up, far away; Ruth says, *It's me . . . I'm okay . . .* Then nothing. They're talking, she's listening. We watch her. She begins to cry. Tears stream down her cheeks, tears that become wrenching sobs, twisting her shoulders, and her upper body, petrified until now, begins to shake as she laughs and cries and tells us, *Tom's alive!* We feel as if we've just witnessed a resurrection. She says a few more words to whoever's on the line, then hands the phone to Hélène. She shakes her head gently, repeating softly for us, for herself, for the earth and sky, *He's alive* . . . Then she turns to Delphine, who's sitting next to her, weeping. Ruth looks at her, lays her head on her shoulder, and Delphine takes her in her arms.

4

It took us a long time to get to Matara, Hélène tells me that night. It's not far, but the road was often washed out, the van kept stopping for hitchhikers, and it had to wait at every bridge because bodies were being fished out of all the rivers. At one point the van drove past the club where we'd planned to go out diving the day of the wave; there was nothing left of the building or the vacation resort it served, and when Hélène asked a policeman what had happened to the hundreds of guests there, he'd sighed and told her, *All dead.* The hospital in Matara was much bigger than the one in Tangalla; they were dealing with many more corpses, and the smell of death was even stronger there. Hélène and Jérôme were taken to the cold room: twenty drawers containing whites—the VIP section, cracked Jérôme grimly. The drawers were opened for them, one by one. Hélène didn't know what she

feared more, finding Juliette in a drawer or not finding her.
She wasn't there. They searched the hospital from top to bottom. Jérôme kept waving the Tangalla "receipt" with the scribbled description of Juliette at people, who gestured sadly and
helplessly at the swollen gray bodies lying everywhere on the
floors: There they are, take your pick . . . After an hour of looking
everywhere, they felt completely at a loss. Someone directed them
to an office where a man sat at a computer running a slide show.
The monitor flashed photos of the dead who'd been brought to
the hospital and sent on elsewhere. A half dozen Sri Lankans
crowding around the screen made room for Hélène and Jérôme,
whom they probably took for a bereaved couple, a handsome couple: a tall man with curly hair in a white shirt, unshaven; a stunning
woman in white pants and a T-shirt—both of them worn out by
grief and worry. Everyone there was grief-stricken, but Hélène
and Jérôme inspired particular sympathy, and the others seemed
eager to help them. Jérôme described his daughter to the hospital
employee, who listened intently but didn't understand too well
and continued streaming the photos. Men and women, young and
old, Sri Lankans and Westerners, photographed full face, their
features battered, swollen, eyes open or closed. Dozens, each image
stopping for a few seconds before the next one automatically
replaced it. Finally, Juliette appeared. Hélène was at Jérôme's
side. She watched him see the photo of his dead little girl. She
watched him stare at it. When Juliette's photo vanished and
another took its place, Jérôme panicked, grabbed the computer,
and shouted for someone to make the slide show go backward.
The employee clicked the mouse, then checked the information
listed with the photo: Juliette was no longer there, she'd been
sent to Colombo the previous evening. Her photo vanished
again, and again Jérôme went wild, pleading to go back once
more—he couldn't turn away from the screen, couldn't accept

Juliette's disappearance. As the employee clicked repeatedly to reverse the slide show, Jérôme gazed greedily at his daughter's face, at her blond hair, the straps of her red sundress on her round, tanned shoulders. Each time the next photo appeared, he begged, Again! Again, again!—and writing this, I think of Jeanne, our own little girl, who has recently learned to say *Encore!* non-stop to prolong a game of "This is the way the ladies ride." Was it Hélène who did what needed to be done? Taking his hand to tear him away from that abyss, saying, Come on, let's go, we have to go . . . How did they get back here? There were gaps in her story, and she spoke with some reticence. True, she was exhausted, at the end of her tether, but I also understood that if she didn't tell me everything, it was so as not to betray the awful and wrench-ing intimacy she had just shared with Jérôme, an intimacy that wounded me.

Another day passed before we could leave for Colombo. An empty day: there was nothing left to do but wait, and we waited. We kept to ourselves, so I hardly remember who else was around. On the periphery, almost invisible because they ate somewhere apart from everyone else, were the Swiss German Ayurvedics and Leni Riefenstahl, who still swam her laps every morning. We saw an Israeli couple fussing over their daughter; she was about Juliette's age, and they were obviously only too aware that she could have met the same fate as Juliette. There was also an unpleas-ant French family carrying on about their lost credit cards and what the wrong people might do if they got their hands on them. As for their cash, they'd already given up on that, they announced, admiring their ability to roll with the punches. They probably resented Delphine and Jérôme, whose tragedy put a damper on their recital of woe; they avoided them, in any case, and only in their absence would they swoop down on Hélène or me to borrow a cell phone and yell at their insurance company to send a helicopter for them immediately.

Jérôme persuaded the hotel management to arrange transportation the next day to Colombo. The minibus could accommodate a dozen passengers, tightly packed, and part of the evening was spent trying to decide who'd get the seats. There would be another departure in a day or two, perhaps, but it wasn't definite, and since most of the available vehicles had been requisitioned for rescue work and fuel was scarce, we seized the opportunity. Jérôme, Delphine, and Philippe had priority, of course, and we had been so close to them from the very first day that we were naturally on the list as well. Jean-Baptiste and Rodrigue had been going crazy doing the bungalow–restaurant–swimming pool circuit, so they were relieved to be going. Ruth had learned from her family that Tom was hospitalized in a town about fifty kilometers inland, in the mountains. No one could figure out how he had wound up there, but since great chunks of the coastal road were cut off and we'd have to reach Colombo by going up-island, it was agreed that we'd make a detour to take her to him. That left four seats the management felt obliged to offer to the disagreeable French family, but either the prospect of their grieving compatriots' company distressed them or they were convinced a helicopter was on the way from their insurance company, because luckily they declined.

The night before we set off, Ruth joined our group for dinner, which I remember, as does Jean-Baptiste, as the strangest time of that entire week. If I try to describe it, I'm forced to evoke a kind of euphoria—tragic and frenetic, yes, but euphoric all the same. We drank a lot. Beer, but also wine, the kind you find on the wine list of a restaurant in southern Sri Lanka, something akin to a five-year-old Beaujolais Nouveau bottled by a South African Tamil wine merchant and corked to boot. This frightening rotgut, several bottles of which we nevertheless dispatched (the entire supply, in fact), provoked withering scorn from Philippe and Jérôme, devotees of the *grands crus bordelais* now goaded by the pathetically indecipherable label on this swill into an outburst of complete nonsense stuffed with their favorite jokes and associations—plonk, rock 'n' roll, the hazelnut aftertaste of a Château Cheval Blanc, Keith Richards stories—all compounded by the pretensions of the Swiss German Ayurvedics, with whom Jérôme, on a roll, amused himself by insulting zestfully every time one went by: How's it going, feeling serene? Seriously Zen? Swinging along on the path to liberation? That's great, guys, really great, hang in there! He was in a ferociously sarcastic mood, but it was with real affection that he had us all drink to Tom's resurrection. Ruth was clearly uncomfortable. Imprisoned in her own pain a few hours earlier, drifting far from the world of the living, she had lost all consciousness of others; no one existed except for her dead Tom—and his wife, determined to die of grief. Since the miracle of the telephone call, however, she had again become what she must have been all her life, a sweet, compassionate young woman whose instinct was to restrain her joy and share the sorrow of these people who had kindly come to her aid. But she'd never encountered anything like Jérôme's furious vitality. He ate nothing, but he drank, smoked, laughed, teased, and talked loudly, refusing to let silence fall. We had to bear up, and he bore up. He carried everything, lifted us all, swept us along in his wake. At the same time, out of the corner of his eye, he kept watch over Delphine, and I remember thinking, there it is, real love, a man who truly loves his wife. There's nothing more beautiful. But Delphine remained silent, absent, horribly calm. It was as if Jérôme and Philippe—because Philippe was valiantly backing up his son-in-law—were doing a sacred dance around her, as if they were constantly calling to her: Don't go, we're begging you, stay with us! Sitting next to Delphine, Ruth took her hand several times, timidly, as if she hadn't the right, and tenderly because she did have the right after all, or because no one had the right, or everyone did, or there was no "right" anymore, there were no more proprieties to observe, nothing left but this elegant blond mass of pain for which there was no remedy, and the need to take her hand.

It was late, toward the end of this dinner, when Rodrigue, dead tired, slipped onto Hélène's lap. Like the little boy he still was, he nestled his head against her shoulder, and she stroked his hair for a long time. She petted him, reassured him: I'm here. Then she took him off to bed. As they left through the garden, Delphine watched them go. What was she thinking about? Her little girl, whom she'd petted and tucked into bed only four nights ago and would never pet and tuck into bed again? Was she thinking about how she'd never again sit on her child's bed to read her a story? Never, ever, arrange all her stuffed animals around her again? For the rest of her life, stuffed animals, cute mobiles, and the sound of music boxes would tear at her heart. *How is it possible that this woman can be hugging her living child while my little girl is so cold and will never speak or move again?* How could she not hate them, Hélène and her child? How could she not pray, *Dear God, perform a miracle; give me back mine and take hers. Make her be the one to hurt the way I do and make me be like her, full of that comfortable, cushioned sadness that simply helps others to better enjoy their own good fortune.*

Delphine looked away from the silhouettes of Hélène and Rodrigue melting into the dark path to the bungalows. When our eyes met briefly, she smiled and murmured, He's so little . . .

The distance was immense, the gulf between us impossible to bridge, but there was kindness in her halting voice, and tenderness, and it was this sweetness more than my morbid thoughts that gave me the shivers. With hindsight, I feel that something extraordinary happened that evening. We were with a man and a woman who had just experienced the worst thing that can ever happen to the human soul, while we had escaped unscathed. And yet, even if certain thoughts lurked in the back of their minds— and they certainly had such thoughts—and if they could have changed places, saving themselves by plunging us into misfortune, they would have, anyone would have, we all prefer our own children to those of others, it's only human, *and yet*, I think on that evening, during that dinner, they did not resent us. They did not hate us, as I had feared they would. They rejoiced like us in the miracle that had just restored to Ruth the joy that had been forever taken from them. Delphine was moved by the sight of Rodrigue cradled in his mother's arms. We experienced these moments together. For a few days we were as intimately connected and as radically separated as it is possible to be. I know that we loved them and I believe that they loved us.

We left the restaurant quite late, Hélène and I. Abandoning the last sounds of conversation, we followed the paved path beside the swimming pool and stepped into the shadows beneath the immense trees. The hotel grounds were extensive; it was a five-minute walk from the main building to our bungalow, five minutes that acted like an air lock. The only sound now was the constant peaceful chirring of insects, and when you looked up, the sky above the coconut palms was so full of stars you thought you could hear them trilling, too. Invisible waves broke rhythmically on the beach down below. We walked in silence, exhausted.

We knew that soon we'd be lying side by side, and our tense bodies began preparing themselves for sleep. We held hands.

When I think back on that time, I remember my childish fear that Hélène would turn away from me, but what she herself remembers is that we were together, truly together.

5

On the morning we left, the remaining seats in the minibus wound up being assigned to a few Swiss German Ayurvedics, who obviously knew what had happened to Delphine and Jérôme and, by never mentioning it, probably thought they were being genuinely considerate. They simply greeted us en masse with a quick nod, and when they saw Jérôme—who was sitting up front—light a cigarette, they informed us that even with the windows open the smoke bothered them. Our trip instantly became an endless series of cigarette stops, with everyone leaving the bus except the Ayurvedics, who couldn't complain, being in the minority, but clearly figured we were purposely trying to piss them off. On the first leg, we drove to Galle along the coastal road, making fitful progress because of obstructions and rescue convoys.

Processions of survivors trudged along the roadside, and we wondered where they were going with their bundles and handcarts. As we approached the city, traffic slowed even more, but the crowds disappeared once the minibus took the road into the mountains. Leaving the front lines behind, we drove through peaceful and luxuriant landscapes. Villagers tending casually to their affairs waved and smiled at us. The countryside looked just as it had to Jérôme and Philippe on their scouting trip of twelve years earlier, as if nothing had happened, as if here, far from the coast, no one even knew about the wave at all.

During one of our smoking breaks by the side of the road, Philippe took me aside and asked, So, you're a writer. Are you going to write a book about this?

His question took me by surprise. I hadn't thought about it. I replied that as far as I knew, no.

You ought to, Philippe insisted. Me, if I could write, I'd do it.

Then do it. You're in a better position to write it than I am.

Philippe looked at me skeptically, but within a year he did do it, and did it well.

After the hospitals in Tangalla and Matara, the one in Ratnapura, about a hundred kilometers southeast of Colombo, was a comfort to visit. Here the staff was treating patients, not triaging the dead. Instead of corpses on the floor, there were injured people in beds or, for the latest arrivals, on straw pallets cluttering the halls, making it hard to move around. That Tom should have turned up fifty kilometers from the coast seemed inexplicable, almost supernatural, but it wasn't the wave that had brought him here. The explanation was more prosaic: people for whom something could still be done had been evacuated inland to this hospital. Some were horribly wounded; we heard patients moaning and gasping for breath. There were shortages of drugs and bandages, medical personnel were clearly overwhelmed—it was like being in a field hospital in wartime. I don't know how many doors we opened before Ruth froze on a threshold, signaling Hélène and me to wait. Having spotted Tom, she wanted to make the moment last, to look at him while he was still unaware of her presence. There were twenty or so beds; she pointed out his. He was staring straight ahead. A big fellow with close-cropped hair and bandages wrapped around his bare chest. He didn't know that Ruth was there or even that she was alive, just as she'd been in the dark about him the day before. Finally, she approached him. She entered his field of vision. They remained motionless for a moment, silently facing each other, he propped up against pillows, she standing at the foot of the bed, and then she moved into his arms. Everyone in the room was watching; many began to cry. It did them good to cry because a man and a woman in love who'd believed each other dead had been reunited. It felt good to see these two look at each other and touch each other with such amazement. Tom's chest had been staved in and one lung perforated, a serious injury, but he was being well cared for. On his bedside table were a tattered spy novel, a few cans of beer, and a bunch of grapes, all brought by a toothless old man whom Tom didn't know but who was looking after him. Every day since Tom's arrival, the little man had brought him similar small gifts, and he was right there, sitting modestly on the edge of the bed. Tom introduced him to Ruth, who embraced him gratefully. Then Ruth walked outside with Hélène and me to the parking lot where the others were waiting and said good-bye to everyone. As soon as Tom could travel, they would go home. Their story would have a happy ending.

* * *

Hélène, as I mentioned, never found the piece of paper with Ruth and Tom's phone number. We never knew their last name, so it's unlikely we'll ever find out what has happened to them. As I write this, more than three years have passed. If they've stuck to their plan, they should be living in the house that Tom built, with their child. Perhaps they've had two already. Do they ever talk about the wave? About those terrible days when each thought the other dead and their own lives washed away? Are we part of their story, the way they are part of ours? What do they remember of us? Our first names? Our faces? As for their faces, I've forgotten them. Hélène tells me Tom's eyes were very blue and Ruth was beautiful. She thinks of them sometimes, mostly to hope with all her heart that they're happy and will grow old together. Of course, in hoping that, she's thinking about us.

The French embassy in Colombo sent us to the Alliance Française, which was operating as a welcome center offering support to tourists affected by the catastrophe. They'd set up mattresses in classrooms and posted lists of the missing in the lobby, lists that grew by the day. Psychiatrists offered their services. Delphine had calmly agreed to see one, who later confided his concern to Hélène: Delphine was bearing up *too* well, refusing to allow herself to break down, which would make her inevitable collapse upon returning home all the more massive. There was something unreal, even anesthetizing about the present atmosphere of disaster, but soon reality would catch up with her. Hélène nodded; she knew the psychiatrist was right. She thought about the little girl's room back home in Saint-Émilion, about the moment when Delphine would enter that room. To postpone that moment, we would almost have preferred not to leave, not right away, not just yet, instead staying together a little longer in the eye of the cyclone, but our departure was already being organized, with talk of seats on a plane taking off the next morning. Jérôme had himself driven, alone this time, to the hospital where Juliette's body had been taken. When he returned, he told Delphine that she was lovely, undamaged, and then confessed to Hélène with a sob that he had lied to Delphine: in spite of the cold room, she was decomposing. His little daughter was decomposing. Then there was a whole muddle about the cremation. Delphine and Jérôme wanted to take the body home, but not for burial. When everything is absolutely unbearable, something, some detail, always manages to be more unbearable than all the rest, and for them it was the image of a little coffin. They did not want to walk behind the little coffin of their daughter. They wanted to have her cremated in France, but the authorities explained to them that this was not possible. For sanitary reasons, the body would have to be repatriated in a lead casket, soldered shut, which could neither be opened again nor incinerated. If they took it home, they would have to bury it. The other solution, if they wanted to cremate the body, was to do it at the hospital, and after a long and stormy discussion Juliette's parents resigned themselves to that. It was already dark when Jérôme and Philippe went to the hospital. They came back much later with an already half-empty bottle of whiskey that we polished off, and then we drank some more at a restaurant they knew, where they always dined ritually on the first evening of every visit to Sri Lanka. When closing time came, the manager agreed to sell us one more bottle. It helped us stay awake until it was time to take the plane, which we boarded drunk. We fell asleep immediately.

* * *

What I remember of that last night in Colombo is a feeling of panic, confusion, and despair. At one point, a Buddhist ceremony was under consideration, and then it wasn't. The cremation was done on the fly, a dirty job you couldn't invite anyone to attend, after which there was nothing left to do but get drunk and get out. We might have stayed one day longer, tried to do things properly, but that didn't mean anything, doing things properly: nothing made sense anymore, nothing could be right anymore, we had to finish it, just get it done, and not even properly. By dawn, at the airport, Jérôme with his quiet strength had turned into a kind of sneering punk with bloodshot eyes, taunting the other passengers, and if anyone so much as made a sound, he screamed in their faces, My daughter's dead, fuckhead, you got that?

I remember something else, though. We'd just arrived at the Alliance Française, where they'd asked if we wanted to take showers. Had the water been cut off or even rationed at the Hotel Eva Lanka after the wave? I don't think so. We'd had a long day of traveling, that's all, but it was as if we'd emerged from the desert after three months without washing. The children took their showers first, then Hélène and I, together. We stood facing each other for a long time under the thin trickle of water. We had a sense of how fragile our bodies were. I looked at Hélène's, so lovely, so weighed down with horror and fatigue. I felt not desire but a searing pity, a need to care, to cherish, to protect forever. I thought, She might have died. She is precious to me. So precious. I'd like her to be old someday, I'd like her flesh to be old and flabby, and I'd like to still love her. Everything that had happened in those five days and was ending then, at that precise moment, washed over us. A dam opened, releasing a flood of sorrow, relief, love, all mixed together.

I hugged Hélène and told her, I don't want to break up anymore, not ever.

She said, I don't want to break up anymore either.

6

―

Two weeks after we got back to Paris I found the apartment we still live in. Several days later, the lease signed, we were inspecting the place with the Polish contractor who would be remodeling our kitchen when Hélène's cell phone rang. She said hello, listened for a few moments, then went into the next room. When the contractor and I rejoined her, she was teary-eyed and her chin was trembling. Her father had just told her that Juliette had cancer again—again, because she'd already had cancer as an adolescent. This I knew. What else did I know about her then? That she used crutches, that she was a judge, and that she lived near the city of Vienne, in the *département* of Isère. Hélène rarely saw her sister; their lives were quite different, and there was always something more pressing to do than visit Vienne. But Hélène loved her. She spoke of her with tender affection and even admiration. Just before the Christmas holidays, Juliette had suffered a pulmonary embolism; Hélène had been worried, but the tsunami had swept that worry away along with the rest of our former life, and there'd been no further cause for concern since our return. Now, though, she had cancer again. Of the breast, this time, with metastases to the lungs.

We went to see her one February weekend, at the beginning of her chemotherapy. Knowing her hair would soon fall out, she'd asked Hélène to get her a wig, so Hélène had made the rounds of the shops to find the most attractive one. She'd also bought dresses for Juliette's three daughters. Anything to do with elegance, style, or flair—that's Hélène's department. It was clearly not Juliette's or her husband's: they were living in a modern single-family home in a charmless village, half country, half suburb. Walking in, I saw an exhausted woman who'd lost weight and no longer left her armchair; a handsome, slender, gentle husband, perhaps a bit of a dreamer; and three truly ravishing little girls, the eldest of whom—she was seven—drew sketchbooks full of princesses in royal robes and jeweled crowns, with a care and sureness of line I found astonishing for her age. She was just as serious about her dance lessons, though she laughed along when I improvised some clumsy entrechats with her to the strains of *Swan Lake.* But apart from these welcome shenanigans, a mixture of unease and laziness kept me on the sidelines of the conversation, which Juliette's weakness somewhat hampered in any case. The winter afternoon dragged by; we soon turned on the lamps. As I always do when I arrive somewhere, I inspected the reading material on offer: a small bookcase held textbooks, children's books, essays for the general public on bioethics and the law, plus a few novels of the kind one buys for a long trip. In this (to me) depressing array I spotted a more promising book, a novel by Béatrix Beck, whom I like a lot: *Plus loin: mais où?* (Farther Away: But Where?). Leafing through it, I came across a sentence that made me laugh, and I read it aloud to everyone: "A visit always brings pleasure—if not when it begins, then when it ends."

Juliette wasn't eager for us to visit again too quickly—not until she'd recovered from the chemotherapy, she said. Two months passed, during which she and Hélène spoke only on the phone. Juliette being the type who reassures those close to her so as not to upset them, the news was all the more worrying. The doctors, she said, were optimistic. The combination of the chemo and a new therapy, Herceptin, seemed to be beating back the cancer. They were talking about a remission, however, not a cure, and even if Juliette hoped it would be a long one, her life was now reduced to this remission. When Hélène offered to come see her, Juliette replied, Let's wait a bit, wait till the weather's nice and we can be in the garden, that'll be more pleasant, and anyway . . . just now I'm too tired. These conversations tore Hélène apart. She'd tell me, in a kind of stupor, My little sister's going to die. Maybe in six months or a year, but it's definite, she's dying. I'd take Hélène in my arms, I'd cradle her face in my hands, saying, I'm here, and it's true, I was there. I remembered how a year earlier the eldest of my own sisters had almost died, and the youngest as well, many years before: those memories helped me feel a little of what Hélène was going through, helped me to be a little more present, but except at those moments when she was talking about Juliette's fate, or when she wasn't but I saw that she'd been crying, the truth is that I hardly thought about it at all. Aside from that distant threat, our life was happy. To celebrate our new home, we threw a huge party, and for several weeks afterward all our friends kept telling us that parties as joyful as that one were rare indeed. I was proud of Hélène's beauty, of her sharp wit, her generosity of character, and I loved, not feared, her streak of melancholy. The film I'd shot the previous summer was going to be shown at the Cannes Film Festival. I felt brilliant, important, and this quasi-sister-in-law with cancer off in her little house in the backwater of her dumpy province, well, I was sorry about her plight, of course, but from afar. That particular life on its way out had nothing to do with my life, in which everything seemed to be opening, unfolding. What bothered me the most was that worry was eating away at Hélène and thus keeping me (although hardly at all, actually) from freely displaying, in her presence, the slightly manic euphoria that cheered me all that spring.

Between Cannes and the official opening of the film, there was one more stop on my path to glory: another festival, in Yokohama. I'd fly business class; the cream of the French film world would be there, and I already saw myself receiving kudos in Japanese. Hélène was working, so she couldn't go with me, but she planned to hop down at last to Vienne while I was gone. Juliette was saying she felt somewhat better; there'd be mild weather, they could sit out in the garden. I was to leave on Monday, and on Friday I recorded the voice-over for a documentary I'd shot with a friend in Kenya. I was doing lots of things and felt I could go on forever. Recording my voice, mastering it better than I do in real life—this always brought me a narcissistic thrill, and I'd managed to fit into the commentary the sentence that made me laugh, the one about how visits always bring pleasure, if not when they begin, then when they end, so I and my editor, Camille, left the studio quite content with ourselves and our afternoon. We went off to a café for a drink. I bummed a cigarette from a girl at the next table; she made a joke, so did I, and Camille—who's always a great audience for me—laughed delightedly, and that's when my cell phone rang. It was Hélène. She was calling from the TV station and leaving directly to catch a train: Juliette was dying.

When we got off the train at the Gare de Perrache in Lyon, Hélène's parents were waiting for us. They'd hurriedly left the house in Poitou where they were spending a few days on vacation and had just driven east all the way across France. I thought at the time that they'd waited to call Hélène until they'd covered at least half the distance, so that she wouldn't arrive before they did, but I later discovered, back at our apartment, a series of increasingly urgent messages on our answering machine, which reminded me of the ones I'd found on mine twenty years earlier, when my youngest sister was in a serious car accident. I'd returned home too late and too drunk to listen to my messages and heard them only the next morning. The horror of the news was compounded (even if it didn't change a thing) by the shame of having been unduly shielded from it all night long, of having slept the sleep of the drunk—if not the just—even though my mother, whom I've often accused of keeping silent about the truth to protect her family, had done everything she could to reach me. As Hélène and I settled into the backseat of her parents' car, I had the feeling things were following a pattern long since abandoned: grown-ups in front, children in back. The ride to the Hôpital de Lyon-Sud was fairly long, with endless detours, signs we'd see too late, and exit ramps we couldn't take in time, so we'd take the next one, then the service road back in the other direction. Dealing with these navigational difficulties gave us something neutral to talk about. For Hélène's parents (and mine), good manners begin with keeping one's feelings to oneself, but their eyes were red and Jacques, her father, gripped the wheel with shaking hands. Just before we arrived, Marie-Aude, her mother, said without turning around that this would probably be the last time we'd see Juliette. Maybe there'd be another chance tomorrow, but no one knew for certain.

Juliette was in the intensive care unit. Hélène and her parents entered the room; I hung back at the threshold, but Hélène motioned for me to come in and stand behind her, close by, while she took her sister's hand, tethered to an intravenous needle. At her touch, Juliette, who'd been lying motionless with her head tilted back, turned slightly toward Hélène. Her lungs were failing; all the energy Juliette had left was devoted to the now horribly difficult task of breathing. She'd lost her hair and her face was waxen, emaciated. I'd seen my first dead people in Tangalla, a great many of them all at once, but I had never watched anyone die. Now, I was watching. Juliette's parents and sister all spoke to her; she was unable to answer but looked at them and seemed to recognize them. I don't remember what they said. Probably her name, who they were, that they were there. Juliette, it's Papa. Juliette, it's Mama. Juliette, it's Hélène. And they squeezed her hands, touched her face. Suddenly, she sat up, arching her back. She grabbed roughly, clumsily, at the oxygen mask, trying to tear it off, as if it were impeding her breathing instead of helping her. Panicking, we thought it had stopped working, that Juliette would die for lack of air before our eyes. A nurse rushed in and told us no, the machine was working properly. Hélène, who was supporting Juliette in her arms, helped her lie back on the bed again, like a recumbent figure on a tomb. Juliette did not resist; starting up like that had exhausted her. She seemed not so much calm as distant, out of reach. The four of us stayed for a minute more at her bedside. The nurse then told us that during the afternoon, when she could still speak, Juliette had asked to see her daughters, but only after their school's end-of-the-year celebration, a festive program that would take place the next morning. The doctors thought they could keep her alive until then and would see that she got some rest later that night. All this had been worked out by Juliette and her husband. She didn't want to die stupefied by drugs, yet she was relying on them to keep terrible suffering from stealing her death. She wanted help in hanging on long enough to do what she had left to do, but nothing more. The nurse was impressed not only by her courage but even more by her lucidity and determination.

That night, in the hotel, Hélène lay next to me, but she was walled off and, like her sister, out of reach. Every so often she would get up to smoke a cigarette near the half-open window, and I would get up to join her. It was a nonsmoking room, so we used a plastic cup from the bathroom as an ashtray, with a little water in it so it wouldn't melt. The water became a disgusting brew. We both intended to stop smoking and had already racked up a few failed attempts to quit, so we'd agreed that instead of trying and failing and getting discouraged, we'd wait for a favorable—that is, less stressful—opportunity to stop for good. For me this meant after my film had come out, and for Hélène (I now realize, even if we never said so), after Juliette's death, which she'd been anticipating for several months, paralyzed by anguish. We were getting up, smoking, going back to bed, getting up again—all in near silence. At one point Hélène said, It's good that you're here, and her saying that helped me. At the same time, I was thinking of Yokohama, telling myself that the odds of my taking the plane on Monday weren't great and then trying to figure out how slim they really were. I was thinking about Sri Lanka, too, about the way Hélène and I had embraced in the shower at the Alliance Française and resolved never to part.

Her parents' room was three doors down from ours. Neither they nor my parents had ever been separated. Jacques and Marie-Aude were growing old together, and while we didn't see them as role models, I thought that was something, growing old together. They must have been lying on their bed, in silence. Maybe they were lying close together. Maybe they were turned toward each other, crying. It was their child's last night, or just about. She was thirty-three. They'd come here for her death. And the three little girls, a few kilometers away? Were they asleep? What was going through their heads? What does it mean, when you're seven, to know your mother is dying? And when you're four? One? People say a one-year-old doesn't know, doesn't understand, but even without words a child must sense that something serious is going on, that life is in upheaval and will never be truly safe again. Something was bothering me, a question of language: I hate hearing the word *mama* used other than in private and in direct address. That even a sixty-year-old would address his or her mother as "Mama"—fine. But when anyone past kindergarten age says "So-and-so's mama" or, like former presidential candidate Ségolène Royal, talks about "the mamas," I feel a disgust that goes beyond the snobbishness that makes me wince when someone says "No problem" or "The thing of it is, is that . . ." And yet even for me, the dying woman was not the mother of Amélie, Clara, and Diane but their mama, and this word that I dislike and that makes me sad, well, I won't say it didn't sadden me, but I had a longing to say it, softly, *mama*, and to cry and be, not consoled, no, but gently rocked, just rocked, and to fall asleep like that.

7

Rosier, where Juliette, Patrice, and their three daughters lived and where Patrice and the girls still do, is a tiny village without shops or a café, but it has a church and a school around which housing developments have sprung up. The church probably dates to the end of the nineteenth century, but nothing else around it does, so one wonders what Rosier once looked like. Perhaps it was a farming village before these young couples who work in Vienne or Lyon moved in, drawn there because it was a fine place to raise children and not too expensive. When we'd visited Juliette in February, Rosier had reminded me unpleasantly—both the place and the people—of where Jean-Claude Romand and his family had lived, not far from there, in the Pays de Gex.* The vil-

---

* Jean-Claude Romand is the subject of Carrère's *The Adversary: A True Story of Monstrous Deception*. For eighteen years Romand pretended to be a doctor and consultant at the World Health Organization when in reality he had never finished medical school

lage seemed more attractive in June, especially since the weather
was pleasant. Patrice and Juliette's yard, with its swing and plastic
pool, looked out onto the church square. I imagined the girls
leaving after breakfast with their backpacks, the snacks after they
came home from school, the visits from one neighbor to another,
the bicycles hanging in everyone's garages over the workbench
and the lawnmower. A little parochial, but still, it was a pretty
picture.

There were lots of people in the house when we arrived that
Saturday morning: Patrice and his daughters, who were getting
ready for their big event at school, but also parents and siblings
from both sides of the family, as well as neighbors dropping in for
a few minutes and a cup of coffee. That last was in continual
preparation, so cups needed to be retrieved from the not-yet-
started dishwasher and rinsed out in the sink. As the most recent
arrival, I needed a task and sat down at the kitchen table to help
Patrice's mother prepare a large salad for lunch. We all knew why
we were there, so there was no point in talking about it, but then
what could we talk about? Patrice's mother had read my book
The Adversary (which Juliette had recommended to her, explaining that I was Hélène's fiancé) and found it a hard story to read. I
allowed as how yes, it was hard, and that it had been hard to
write, too, and I felt vaguely ashamed of writing such hard things.
In my circle, people have no problem with a dark book or a perverse subject; many even find special merit in such things, proof
of the author's audacity. Less sophisticated readers like Patrice's
mother are perturbed and perplexed. They don't consider it
wrong to write such things, but they still wonder why anyone

---

and was supporting his family by bilking friends and relatives through a Ponzi scheme.
In 1993, fearing exposure, Romand killed his wife and two children, his parents, their
dog, *and* quite possibly his father-in-law and tried to murder his mistress. He is currently in prison.

would. They tell themselves that the affable, well-mannered guy helping slice cucumbers, who seems to be sincerely joining in the family mourning, must nevertheless be really twisted or really unhappy, because there's something wrong with him, and the worst thing is, I have to admit they're right.

I was hiding out all the more willingly in the company of Patrice's mother because I didn't dare approach the girls, the two oldest, that is, Amélie and Clara. Being genial and polite wasn't enough with them. I didn't know what I ought to do, but I knew I couldn't do it at the moment. The first time I'd visited I'd played the clown and made Amélie laugh. Antoine was currently doing that job. Antoine is Hélène and Juliette's younger brother, one of the easiest people to love that I know. He's cheerful, friendly, there's nothing constrained or defensive about him, and he puts everyone immediately at ease, particularly children. Later I discovered how deeply he felt sorrow and pain, but that day I envied him his simplicity, his straightforward attitude toward life, such a contrast with my own character—and Hélène's, I thought at the time. Hélène, however, is able to give of herself to others. I'd discovered that watching her help the survivors of the tsunami, and I noticed it again seeing her with Clara. According to his mother, Patrice had spoken to his three girls the day before. And that meant he'd told them, Mama's going to die, so tomorrow, after the school festival, all four of us will go see her, and it will be for the last time. He had said those words and probably repeated them. And Clara had understood them. She knew that at the age of four she was going to lose her mother's irreplaceable love, and she was already seeking a substitute in her aunt. I watched Hélène caressing her, dealing with her wheedling and her tears, and I was deeply moved by her exquisite tact, just as I'd been impressed by her in Sri Lanka, in precisely the opposite situation, consoling the parents of a different Juliette.

* * *

I have been and still am a scriptwriter; constructing dramatic situations is one of the things I do, and a cardinal rule of the profession is not to be afraid of audacious excess and melodrama. Still, I don't think I would ever have dared, in making up a story, to stage as shameless a tearjerker as a scene of two little girls dancing and singing at their school festival as their mother lies dying in the hospital. While we waited for them to come on, about every ten minutes Hélène and I snuck away from the audience on the benches in the playground to have a cigarette. We'd then rejoin the rest of the family, and when first Clara appeared, in a kindergarten ballet of little fishies underwater, followed by Amélie in a tutu for a hula-hoop number, we waved exuberantly like everyone else to catch their eyes, to show them we were there. They were conscientious, industrious little girls, and their performances were important to them. A few days earlier, they'd believed their mother would be there to see them. When she'd gone to the hospital, Patrice had told them—doubtless still hoping it would be true—that she'd be back in time for the festival. Then, that maybe she wouldn't be able to attend after all but would be home soon. And finally, as of last night, that she would not come home again. What made it all the more wrenching, if that were possible, was that the show was very well done. Really. My sons, Gabriel and Jean-Baptiste, are older now, but I've seen my fair share of kindergarten and elementary school extravaganzas with theatrics, singing, and pantomime, and of course they're always sweet as can be, but they're also tedious, chaotic, a bit of a mess, so that if there's one thing parents appreciate it's when the teachers manage to keep things short. The Rosier school festival was not short, but neither was it held together with baling wire. The little ballets and sketches had a precision reflecting much

work and care, an unthinkable endeavor for the artsy yuppie
schools my sons attended. These children looked happy, at ease.
They were growing up in the countryside, in a protected family
environment. People must have tormented and divorced one
another in Rosier the way they do everywhere else, except that then
they left Rosier, which was truly a place for families, where every
child cavorting onstage could look out at the audience and find
Mama and Papa sitting on a bench together. It was life as it appears
in TV ads, average in all things, devoid not only of style but also
of the sense that style might be something to strive for. I looked
down on that life, I wouldn't have wanted it, but on that day I
watched the children, I watched their parents videotaping them,
and I reflected that choosing life in Rosier meant choosing not only
the safety of the herd but love as well.

In the crowd of parents filling the playground and then gathering
in front of the church after the show, everyone knew. People were
not yet speaking of Juliette in the past tense, but no one could
pretend to any hope. Neighbors and more or less close friends
would come over and embrace Patrice, who was holding baby
Diane, and squeeze his shoulder, offering to take care of the children or to put up family members who'd arrived for the passing
of his wife, if they needed somewhere to stay. Patrice wore a
pleasant, desolate smile that expressed real gratitude for even the
most conventional displays of sympathy—which conventionality,
of course, didn't mean they weren't sincere—and what struck me,
what has always struck me about him, was his simplicity. He was
there, in shorts and sandals, feeding his tiny daughter her bottle,
and nothing about him said he'd given a thought to any public
show of grief.

The funfair part of the day began. There were stands for prize fishing and archery, pyramids of canned goods to knock down with a tennis ball, a coloring workshop, a raffle, and so on. Amélie had a booklet of raffle tickets to sell, so all her family and a few neighbors bought some but none of us won anything. Since I was with Amélie and Hélène during the drawing, I pretended to pay serious attention, feverishly checking my numbers and exaggerating my disappointment to make her laugh. She did laugh, but in her own way, solemnly, and I tried to imagine how she would remember this day when she was grown up. I try to imagine, as I write, how she'll feel if she ever reads this book. After the fair, the family had lunch in the garden, beneath the big catalpa. It was quite hot; we could hear children behind the hedges, laughing and splashing in inflatable pools. Sitting quietly at a table, Clara and Amélie were making drawings for their mother. If the color went outside the lines, they would frown and start over. When Diane awoke from her nap, Patrice and Cécile, Juliette's other sister, left for the hospital with the three girls. Just before Amélie got into the car, she turned toward the church, made a furtive sign of the cross, and murmured, quickly, Make it so Mama doesn't die.

Hélène's and my turn came at the end of the afternoon. Anticipating that I would be driving, I'd been careful to memorize the directions from the day before and I made it a point of honor to confidently take the correct route. I couldn't do much, but at least I could be a good chauffeur. We went through the same swinging doors, down the same deserted halls with their fluorescent lighting, and waited a long time by the intercom for permission to enter the ICU. When we walked into Juliette's room, Patrice was lying on the bed next to her with his arm under her neck, his face bent over hers. She was unconscious, her breathing labored. To give Hélène a moment alone with her sister, Patrice stepped out into the hall. I watched Hélène sit down on the bed and take Juliette's inert hand in her own, then stroke her face. Some time passed. When she came out of the room, she asked Patrice what the doctors had said. He told her they thought she would die that night, but no one could say how long it would take. They need to help her now, Hélène said. Patrice nodded and went back into the room.

The doctor on call, a bald young man with gold-rimmed glasses and a wary expression, invited us to sit down. There was a blond nurse with him, as welcoming as he was chilly. You must suspect, Hélène said, what I'm here to ask you. His vague gesture meant not so much "yes" as "please go on" and Hélène, whose eyes began to glisten with tears, went on. She asked him how long the whole thing might last; the doctor repeated that it wasn't possible to say but it was a question of hours, not days. Hélène was torn. It's time now, you have to help her, she said again. He replied simply, We have begun to do so. Hélène left him her cell phone number and asked to be called when it was all over.

In the car on the way back from the hospital, Hélène wasn't sure that she'd been clear enough with the doctor or that his answer had been, either. I tried to reassure her: there had been no ambiguity on either side. She also distrusted the zeal of the friendly nurse, who'd spoken of a possible improvement: Juliette, she'd said in a hopeful tone, might last another twenty-four or even forty-eight hours. Hours like that, Hélène felt, would not be welcome. Juliette had said her farewells; Patrice was with her. The time had come. The only thing medicine could do now was make sure he was there when her time ran out.

We stopped in Vienne to buy cigarettes and have a drink at a sidewalk café on the main avenue. It was Saturday evening in a small provincial city; people were strolling outside in shirtsleeves or light dresses, and the smell of summer and the South was in the air. Besides the usual traffic, we saw and heard go by first some local boys on motorcycles, rearing up on their bikes and revving their engines as loud as possible, then a bridal convoy with white veils streaming from the car antennas and horns blowing full blast, and finally a publicity truck announcing a puppet show that evening. It was a contest of champions, the guy yelled over his megaphone, an event not to be missed: Mr. Punch and Winnie-the-Pooh! As at the school festival, the screenwriter in charge seemed to be laying it on a bit thick.

We talked about Patrice. How was he going to manage, alone with his three daughters and no real resources? The comic strips he worked on in his basement office at home didn't bring in much; it had been Juliette's salary as a judge that supported the family, and even though the girls didn't lack for anything, there was a feeling things were tight at the end of the month. Of course the insurance would kick in and the house would be paid off. And Patrice would find work. Gentle and modest, he was no live wire, he wasn't about to open a public relations firm, but you could count on him: everything there was to do, he would do. Eventually, he would remarry. A fellow that nice, that handsome, would naturally find a woman who was equally nice. He would know how to love her the way he'd loved Juliette; there was no morbid streak in Patrice, he wasn't the type to settle comfortably into mourning. So all that would come; no need to rush things. For the moment, he was there, cradling his dying wife, and however long she took, he would surely hold her until the end, until Juliette died safely in his arms. Nothing seemed more precious to me than that security, that certainty of being able to rest until the last moment in the embrace of someone who loves you completely. Hélène had told me what Juliette had said to their sister, Cécile, the previous day, before we arrived, when she could still speak. She'd said she was content: her quiet little life had been a success. At first I thought her words had been words of comfort; then I thought they were sincere, and in the end, true. I remembered Fitzgerald's famous dictum "All life is a process of breaking down," and there I had to disagree. Or at least I didn't think it held true for every life. For Fitzgerald's, perhaps. For mine, perhaps—though I feared that more at the time than I do today. The truth is we don't know what goes on at the last minute; there must be lives that only seem to be failures, that find their meaning in extremis or whose value we have simply missed. There must also be lives that seem a success but are living hells, perhaps even at the end, although that's horrible to imagine. When Juliette passed judgment on her life, however, I believed her, and what led me to believe her is the image of that deathbed on which Patrice held her close. I told Hélène, You know, something happened. Only a few months ago, if I'd learned I had cancer and would soon die, if I'd asked myself the same question as Juliette— has my life been a success?—I could not have given the same answer. I'd have said no, I hadn't made a success of my life. I'd have said I'd succeeded in some things, had two handsome sons who were alive and well, and had written three or four books that gave form to what I was. I had done what I could, with my means and my shortcomings, and I'd fought to do so: that was something, after all. But the essential, which is love, would have escaped me. I was loved, yes, but I had not learned how to love—or hadn't been able to, which is the same thing. No one had been able to rest in complete confidence in my love and I would not rest, at the end, in anyone else's. That's what I'd have said at the news of my impending death, before the wave hit. And then, after the wave, I chose you, we chose each other, and now nothing's the same. You're here, close to me, and if I had to die tomorrow I could say like Juliette that my life has been a success.

8

——

I'm looking at four pages torn from a spiral notebook and filled on both sides with notes describing as precisely as possible Room 304 of the Hôtel du Midi in Pont-Évèque, Isère. I'd been asked to write something for a Festschrift in honor of my friend Olivier Rolin, who the year before had published a novel describing in detail various hotel rooms around the world. Each one provided the setting for a short story, the chief ingredients of which were B-girls, arms dealers, and shady characters with whom the narrator went on epic benders. His publisher had decided to pursue the conceit by enlisting some twenty writers, friends of Olivier's, to describe a hotel room and take it from there, as they pleased. At one point in that interminable night when we were waiting to hear that Juliette had died, to distract Hélène I talked about the project and my hesitation over choosing the hotel. The playful, novelistic tone of the endeavor called for a kind of sophisticated exoticism. In that light, the Hotel Viatka in Kotelnich, Russia, was an apt choice: a classic example of the Brezhnevian style of abandonment, where not a single lightbulb had been changed since the hotel opened and where I spent all told three or four months. At the opposite end of the scale, the only other hotel I'd stayed in for any length of time was the luxurious InterContinental in Hong Kong, where Hélène had joined me during the filming of *The Mustache*. Meeting in the lobby, gazing from our room on the twenty-eighth floor at the panorama of the bay, gliding up and down in the elevators, we might have thought ourselves in *Lost in Translation*. The hotel awaiting me in Yokohama would have been something along those lines, I imagine, and I'd planned as a pleasant vacation exercise to describe my room there. If you don't end up going to Yokohama, said Hélène, you could just describe this room instead. We can do that now, it'll keep us occupied. I grabbed my notebook and we set to work with as much enthusiasm as when we'd rehearsed the erotic scene in my film. I wrote down that the room, approximately 150 square feet, was covered—both walls and ceiling—with yellow wallpaper. Not yellow wallpaper, insisted Hélène, a textured wallpaper imitating a loosely woven fabric that must originally have been white and was then painted yellow. Next we tackled the woodwork, the doorway surrounds, window frames, baseboards, and headboard, all painted a deeper yellow. In short, it was a very yellow space, with accents on the curtains and sheets of the same pink and pastel green found in the room's two pictures, one hanging above the bed and the other on the wall facing it. Printed in 1995 by a company called Nouvelles Images, they betrayed the influence of both Matisse and the *style naïf* of Yugoslavia. Propped up on an elbow, I hastily recorded Hélène's observations as she paced about the room counting the wall sockets, testing the two-way switches, getting caught up in taking inventory. I'll skip the finer points: it was an ordinary room in an ordinary hotel that was, however, well and pleasantly run. The one slightly interesting (and most difficult to describe) feature was in the small entryway. From my notes: "It's a cupboard with double access, one door opening onto the entryway and the other, at a right angle, onto the outside corridor. The equivalent of a serving hatch with two shelves, the upper one for linens, the one below for breakfast trays, as indicated by the pictographs engraved in the glass of two tiny windows that allow you both to understand what should go where and to see if anything's there." I'm not sure that's entirely clear, but so what. We wondered if that kind of cupboard, rarely encountered, had a name that could replace its laborious description. Some people are good at that, they know the names of things in all—or most—categories. Olivier does; I don't; Hélène's a little better. The word *pictograph* in the above lines—I know that was hers.

Dawn arrived. We'd finished our inventory and the phone hadn't rung. The idea that her sister was still hanging between life and death appalled Hélène. I wasn't doing so well either. We closed the curtains, pulled up the covers, and slept badly but a little, close together like spoons. The phone woke us at nine. Juliette had died at four.

We joined Antoine, Jacques, and Marie-Aude for breakfast in the hotel dining room. Cécile was with Patrice and the girls in Rosier. We hugged one another in silence—this silence, when accompanied by a hand patting a shoulder, being the maximal expression of sorrow in our circles. Then we discussed practical matters such as the funeral, who would be where that day, and how to relay one another in the coming days to provide company for Patrice and the girls. Plans were already being made for them to visit this or that household over summer vacation. The next few hours were set: we'd be heading back to Rosier, then to the hospital funeral parlor—I think we simply said "to see Juliette." Not to say our last farewells or to pay our respects to the deceased; our good old-fashioned bourgeois class disdains such euphemisms. When you die you're dead, not deceased or departed, however dearly. Afterward, we were to go to Lyon to see one of Juliette's colleagues. A colleague? On the very day of her death? Hélène and I were surprised. Yes, explained Jacques, a colleague who'd been a judge with her in Vienne and who'd been very close to her during her illness. One of the things that had brought them together was that he, too, had had cancer in his youth, and it had cost him a leg. That morning, on his own initiative, he had invited Juliette's family, since they were all together, to come to his house so that he could talk to them about her. This condolence visit to a one-legged judge struck me as somewhat absurd, but all I had to do was go along.

I don't remember anything about the first meeting with the little girls who'd just lost their mother. I think they were calm, didn't cry; there was no screaming, anyway. Then there was the visit to the hospital funeral parlor, a modern building containing a single huge space with a towering ceiling and lots of light, a kind of atrium reminiscent of the stage settings for classical tragedies and off which opened several smaller areas: viewing rooms, the chapel, the toilets (where one flushed as discreetly as possible, because the whole place was as sonorous as it was silent). We were the only visitors that Sunday morning and were welcomed by a fellow in a white coat who seated us in a corner of the atrium to explain what would be happening in the days leading up to the funeral. He was not, in fact, a medical man, but a volunteer assigned to assist families, and he described succinctly what services the hospital and public agency he represented would handle and what a professional funeral director would provide. Until that professional placed the body in its coffin, the hospital would be in charge of all visits and see to it that the body was brought from the morgue to the viewing rooms and presented as nicely as possible, meaning dressed, coiffed, sometimes made up. All that was free, the families shouldn't hesitate to ask, because people like himself were there to help. On the other hand, especially in the summer, if the funeral was several days away more elaborate cosmetic care might become necessary. That would be provided by the funeral director and would thus cost money. The volunteer was especially careful to explain what was free and what wasn't, repeating himself to make sure he'd been clearly understood, and when I thought about families who were less well off than Juliette's, I found that a good thing. In a speech he must have recited word for word to all families, one sentence kept returning: "We are here to make sure that everything goes as smoothly as possible." No doubt that sentence is a cliché in all professions that deal with death and misfortune, yet one still felt he was really doing what he could to make sure that everything did go as smoothly as possible.

Next we were going to see Juliette, who had been prepared for our visit. Her daughters would come that afternoon. Patrice's mother had thought to have them pick out one of Juliette's favorite dresses, or their own favorite of the ones she'd worn. (In reality, Juliette hardly ever wore a dress, preferring loose, comfortable pants; the clothes she truly cared about were her daughters': the girls had to look like "princesses," that was the word she used, which might well have been why Amélie was always drawing them.) That morning, the two oldest girls had chosen the dress their mama would wear in her coffin, and we'd brought the dress with us so she would have it on when the girls came to see her that afternoon. The volunteer approved of our idea and even announced that fortunately the colleague who would soon take over from him was the acknowledged makeup specialist of their team. Marie-Aude nervously informed him that Juliette had usually worn very little makeup. That was precisely, said the volunteer, why his colleague would be perfect: he would use a light touch and give the impression that she was not made up but alive. When we left the viewing room, after ten minutes about which I have nothing to say, the specialist arrived. Informed of the family's concerns, he took pains to reassure us and asked if one of us, a sister, perhaps, might want to help him apply the deceased's makeup. It's a gesture, he explained, that may seem difficult but that can also do a lot of good. And of course, if at the last minute the person could not go through with it, he would do the job himself, and no harm done. Hélène and Cécile looked at each other without enthusiasm, and in the end neither helped make up her sister. I'm thinking back to that specialist, whom we made fun of a little in the car, Antoine, Hélène, and I: a chubby guy with a lisp in pink Bermuda shorts, who with his dyed hair worn in bangs seemed to be playing a homosexual hairdresser in a theatrical farce, and it's only now, writing this, that I wonder what could have made him volunteer on Sundays to make up corpses, guiding the fingers of their loved ones over the faces. Perhaps, quite simply, the desire to be of help. That's a motive more mysterious to me than plain perversity.

9

I've tried to delay describing our arrival as long as I could, but here we are now, all eight of us, in the one-legged judge's stairwell. The ancient middle-class apartment building is on a pedestrian street that leads to the Gare de Perrache, and I think, That will be convenient if Hélène and I decide to go straight to Paris from here. There's a narrow stone staircase and no elevator, which I find strange for a man with one leg, but fortunately for him it's only one floor up. We ring, the door opens, and we troop in one by one, introducing ourselves and shaking hands with our host, who doesn't notice, now that the stairwell light has automatically switched off, that there's still someone out on the landing—and closes the door in my face. I don't know why but I find it funny (and so does he) that that's how Étienne Rigal and I first met. And I don't know why I'd imagined the one-legged judge as a bachelor living in a tiny dark apartment cluttered with dusty dossiers and smelling, perhaps, of cat. Instead, the apartment was spacious, bright, with attractive, well-cared-for furniture, and there was no need to glance through the half-opened door to a child's bedroom to know that this was a family home. Étienne must have asked his wife and children to go out for a walk, however, because he was by himself. Early forties, tall, well built, in jeans and a gray T-shirt. Prominent and very blue eyes behind rimless glasses. An open face, a soft voice, with the occasional shrill note. When he led us into the living room, we could see that he limped, relying on his right leg to drag the entirely stiff left one along. The room looked out onto the street and sunshine flooded through the windows, bathing the entire floor of handsome old parquet in light. We guests sat down as couples: the parents in a pair of armchairs, Hélène and I close together at one end of a long sofa, Antoine and his wife at the other end, Cécile and her husband on some chairs. There was a bowl full of cherries on a low table, along with a tray of glasses and fruit juices, but when Étienne asked if we wanted coffee, we all said yes, so he went to make some in the kitchen. No one said a word while he was gone. Hélène got up to smoke a cigarette by a window, where I joined her after perusing the bookshelves, which revealed more personal tastes (or interests closer to mine) than those in Rosier. Étienne returned with the coffee. Although he'd used a one-cup espresso machine, all nine cups arrived—mysteriously—piping hot. He asked Hélène for a cigarette, adding, I stopped a long time ago but today is different, I feel scared. We'd all naturally left the armchair facing the sofa free for him because it was in a central position, somewhat like the witness stand in a courtroom, but he preferred to sit on the floor, or rather, to crouch on his right leg with the left one stretched out in front of him, a position that looked fiendishly uncomfortable and that he maintained for almost two hours. We were all looking at him. He looked back at us, one by one, looking at him; I couldn't decide whether he was utterly calm or incredibly keyed up.

He chuckled, to acknowledge his uneasiness, and said, It's strange, isn't it, this situation? It suddenly seems ridiculous to me, and presumptuous, to have made you come like this, as if I had things to tell you that you didn't know about your own daughter, your sister . . . I really am scared, you know. I'm afraid of disappointing you, and of making a fool of myself, which isn't a very dignified fear but, well, that's how I feel. I haven't prepared a speech. Yesterday I tried to sort of compose one in my head, listing the things I wanted to talk about, but that didn't work, I gave up, and anyway I'm not good at that. So I'm just going to say what comes into my head. He was quiet for a moment. There is one thing, he began, I don't think you're aware of and that I'd like you to understand: *Juliette was a great judge.* You know, of course, that she loved her profession and was good at it; you probably think she was an excellent magistrate, but it's more than that. During the five years we worked together at the courthouse in Vienne, Juliette and I, *we were great judges.*

That phrase, and the way he said it, caught my attention. In his voice I heard incredible pride, a pride filled with both apprehension and joy. I recognized the uneasiness; I can spot it in others, from the back, in a crowd, in the dark: they are my brothers. But the joy mixed in with it—that took me by surprise. You sensed that the man speaking was anxious, emotional, always straining toward something just out of reach—but that at the same time he already had what he needed, that he was grounded in an unshakable confidence. This confidence sprang not from serenity or wisdom or mastery but from a way of accepting his fear and using it, a way of *trembling* that made me tremble, too, and understand that something important was happening.

I've quoted Étienne's opening words from memory; they're not literally what he said but close enough. After that, everything is mixed together in my mind, the way everything was mixed together in his narrative. He spoke of justice, of the way Juliette and he dispensed justice. At the court in Vienne, they dealt principally with debt law and housing law: in other words, with cases that pitted the powerful against the impoverished, the strong against the weak, although things were often more complicated—and they liked when that happened, when a dossier was not a series of blanks to fill in but a story and, in the end, a model case. According to Étienne, Juliette would not have liked people to say she was on the side of the poor: that would be too simple, too romantic; above all it would not be juridical and she was above all a jurist. She would have said that she was on the side of the law, but she became—they both became—expert in the art of applying the law justly. To do so they would spend endless hours going through a repayment plan or unearthing a directive no one else would ever have thought of. They would file briefs with the European Court of Justice arguing that the combination of interest rates and penalties charged by certain banks exceeded the usury limit and that this way of bleeding people dry was not only immoral but illegal. Juliette and Étienne's decisions were published, discussed, and violently attacked. The two magistrates were insulted in the *Recueil Dalloz*, the hugely influential series of legal bulletins that publish cases, legislation, and commentary. In judicial circles, the tribunal in Vienne became an important place, a kind of laboratory. People wondered what the hell they'd come up with next, those two little lame judges. Because there was that,

too, of course: they both limped, they'd both survived cancer
when they were adolescents. They'd recognized each other that
first day, fellow cripples, people in whose bodies something had
happened that no one can understand unless they've lived
through it. I've since become familiar with Étienne's way of
thinking and speaking through free associations that owe more,
I imagine, to the experience of psychoanalysis than to any law
school education, but at that first encounter I occasionally got
lost in his sudden leaps from a technical point of law to some
memory—possibly quite personal—of his handicap or Juliette's,
of her illness or his. Cancer had devastated and formed them, and
when it returned to attack Juliette, Étienne had had to confront it
anew as well. A space had opened up, a place near her that neither Patrice nor any family member could fill, only Étienne, and
that place was what he was describing to us. To tell us what? Not
glad tidings. Not that Juliette was brave, or that she fought hard,
or that she loved us, or even that she died happy. Others could
tell us all that. Étienne was talking about something else, something he—and we—found hard to grasp, something baffling that
filled the sunny room with an enormous, crushing presence. And
yet that presence was not a sad one. I felt that presence signaling
to me at a precise moment, when he evoked what for him was the
foundation experience, *the first night*. The first night you spend in
the hospital, alone, having just learned that you're seriously ill and
may die and that from now on, that's your reality. What happens
then, he said, is on the order of all-out war, a complete collapse, a
total metamorphosis. It's a psychic destruction; it can be a refoun-
dation. I don't remember any more of what he said, but I do recall
that when we were saying good-bye, while we were each, out in
the vestibule, shaking his hand, he spoke to me. At no moment
had he shown that he knew I was a writer but there, in front of

everyone, looking me in the eye, he said: You ought to think over what I said about the first night. Perhaps it's something for you.

There we were out on the street, the eight of us, stunned. Hélène and I decided to take the train to Paris, and the others would return to Rosier. We all embraced. We'd see one another again at the funeral. I walked with Hélène to the Gare de Perrache; we crossed the vast place Carnot. Sunday, two in the afternoon, oppressive heat. Middle-class families were dining at home; the poor had claimed the green spaces. While waiting for the train we ate sandwiches at a sidewalk café. We hadn't spoken since leaving the others. What had happened in those last two hours had deeply unsettled but also—it's the only word—thrilled me. I wanted to tell Hélène but was afraid my enthusiasm would seem inappropriate. Besides, I wasn't sure that she liked Étienne as much as I did. At one point, she'd been almost aggressive with him. He'd promised Juliette, he was saying, to take her three daughters on as interns, one after the other. Just a minute, Hélène had said: It's early days yet and we're not going to force them, out of respect for their mother's memory, to become lawyers if they want to do something else. It's not a question of becoming a lawyer, Étienne had replied quietly. I was speaking only about a few days of intern-ship, the kind kids do in high school. Several times, while he was talking, I'd felt Hélène grow impatient next to me and almost rigid. It was like watching a film you love beside someone who's less impressed, and I understood how some of the things Étienne was saying could have antagonized her. Venturing to break the silence by saying I'd found him an extraordinary guy, I fully expected her to reply, A bit self-righteous, though . . . But she didn't say that. She, too, had been moved by Étienne, or rather, she'd been moved by what he'd said about Juliette. Étienne interested her because he had been her sister's friend and confidant. With me it was the opposite: it was because of what he'd said that I was beginning to take an interest in Juliette.

Still, observed Hélène, what he's saying, without saying it, is that he was in love with her.

I said, I don't know about that.

The next night, the first one after Juliette's death, I thought about what Étienne had told us and considered taking up his challenge. Although I later had many doubts about this project and abandoned it for three years (for good, I assumed), that night it clearly seemed like the thing to do. I had received a commission and had simply to accept it. Lying next to a sleeping Hélène, I was enthralled by the idea of a short narrative, something readable in a couple of hours, similar to the time we'd spent with Étienne, a text that would let others share the emotion we'd felt listening to him. The plan, for the moment, seemed quite limited in scope, quite feasible. Technically, I'd have to write it, like *The Adversary*, in the first person—no fiction, no special effects—yet at the same time it would be precisely the opposite of *The Adversary*, its photographic positive, in a way. The events had taken place in the same region, the same social milieu; the people lived in the same kind of houses, read the same books, had the same sort of friends, but on the one side there was Jean-Claude Romand, the incarnation of deception and misfortune, while on the other were Juliette and Étienne, who had relentlessly pursued justice and truth in both their law practice and the ordeal of illness. There was also this coincidence, which bothered me: Hodgkin's lymphoma, the cancer Romand had pretended to have so as to give an acceptable name to the unspeakable thing possessing him, was the one Juliette had had at about the same time, and for real.

Hélène, for her part, decided to write a eulogy to read at the funeral. We talked about it, and I helped her organize her ideas. What she wanted to say was that throughout what Juliette had called her quiet little life, which had been neither quiet nor little, she had always made choices. Juliette never hesitated, never went backward. She made choices and stuck with them: her profession, her husband, her family, their house, their way of living together—she had chosen everything except illness. This life was hers: her place was here and she'd never looked for another one, she'd filled this one completely. There was a point here that was important to Hélène, perhaps in contrast to her feeling that her own life was chaotic. Meanwhile, Hélène was remembering things that didn't seem to make sense, and this upset her. Some people feed those they love; Hélène dresses them. I always wanted to give Juliette a purse, she told me, a lovely handbag, and just as I stepped into the shop I remembered that no, she couldn't carry a handbag because of her crutches. But I could have given her a really nice backpack, instead of the crummy one she had. I could have. I didn't like it that she carried that junk, I didn't give her enough beautiful things. It's horrible—the last present I gave her was that wig. And there was this: when we were little, I was jealous because she was the youngest and the prettiest. Yes, it's true, you saw her only at the end, I'll show you. She went and got some photo albums and spread them out on the kitchen table. I'd already glanced through them with her when we'd unpacked after moving in, but then I'd been paying attention only to Hélène. Now I looked at Juliette: Juliette as a child, a young woman, and it's true, she was pretty.

Prettier than Hélène? That I don't know, I don't think so, but pretty, yes, very, and not at all stern the way I'd imagined her, probably because of her handicap and her job. I looked at her smile, at the crutches never far away, and I didn't see her as brave but as alive, fully and avidly alive. It was after seeing those photos that I spoke to Hélène about my project. I'd feared she might be shocked: her sister, whom I hadn't known, had just died and, bang, I'd decided to do a book about her. She was astonished for a few moments and then decided I was right. Life had brought me to this place, Étienne had defined it for me, and I settled into it.

The next morning at breakfast Hélène laughed heartily and said, You're so funny. You're the only guy I know who could think a friendship between two lame and cancer-ridden judges who pore over debtors' files at the *tribunal d'instance* in Vienne would be a golden opportunity. What's more, they don't even sleep together— and, at the end, she dies. Have I got that straight? That's your story?

Yes, I said. It is.

10

This was my routine: I'd take the eight o'clock train at the Gare de Lyon, pull into Perrache at ten, and be at Étienne's door fifteen minutes later. He'd make coffee. We'd sit down facing each other at the kitchen table, I'd open my notebook, he'd start talking. Years ago, when I was working on *The Adversary*, interviewing people connected to the Romand case, I avoided taking notes in front of them because I feared it might threaten any fragile bonds of confidence I might manage to establish with my subjects. Back at my hotel, I'd transcribe what I remembered of the conversations. With Étienne I had no such concerns. In general I never thought in a "tactical" way with either him or, later, Patrice. I was never afraid of saying the wrong thing or taking the wrong attitude and perhaps alienating the sympathy vital to my endeavor. When I told Étienne at the funeral that I wanted to write about him and Juliette and that now we had to talk, he hadn't seemed at all surprised and simply pulled out his appointment book to propose a date: Friday, July 1. For our project to work he would have to tell me about his life, and he never tried to hide the pleasure that brought him. He liked to talk about himself. It's my way, he said, of talking to and about others, and he remarked astutely that it was my way, too. He knew that in talking about him, I would of necessity be talking about myself. That didn't bother him. Nothing bothered him, I believe, so I felt completely comfortable with the situation as well. It's rather unusual to find yourself talking about not only your past but who you are, what makes you *you* and no one else, to someone you barely know. It happens in the early stages of an affair or in psychoanalysis, and it happened here with disconcerting ease. Étienne's way of talking, as I've said, is free and associative, with abrupt leaps from subject to subject, from one time period to another. I, on the other hand, care intensely about chronology. I find ellipsis acceptable only as a rhetorical device, duly rationed and controlled by me, otherwise I can't stand it. Perhaps because there are snags in the fabric of my life (which I try to repair by keeping the weave as tight as possible), I need to establish markers—such as "the previous Tuesday," "the next night," "three weeks earlier"—and not miss any sections, so in our conversations I kept calling Étienne to order on that point, which requires that I begin this narrative by evoking his father.

Étienne describes him as an atypical academic, curious about everything, who taught first astronomy, then mathematics, statistics, the philosophy of science, and semiology, but because he never settled into one discipline, he missed out on the bright career for which he'd seemed destined. Coming from the hard sciences, he

wished to draw closer to a more human reality and to the uncer-
tainties that come with it. In the sixties he wound up teaching
autoworkers at the Peugeot plant in Montbéliard, where his wife's
family owned a massive, labyrinthine house that was impossible
to heat and eventually had to be sold, to Étienne's lasting regret.
The managers at Peugeot had hired a mathematics teacher to
provide some scientific education, but Étienne's father wanted to
awaken minds by teaching philosophy, politics, and ethics instead.
He was fired after several months, as happened in a number of
places he passed through, leaving his mark on a few noble souls.
He was a typical left-wing Christian, a reader of the French phi-
losophers and social activists Simone Weil and Maurice Clavel,
and a member of the Unified Socialist Party, on whose slate he
ran in the parliamentary elections in Corrèze—the family strong-
hold on the paternal side, this time—against the local conservative bigwig. He lost, but still, he forced a run-off election. A
Christian when with atheists, he became violently anticlerical in
Christian company, perfectly ready to argue that Jesus slept with
his beloved disciple John. At heart, he was a rebel intent on pissing off every level of the establishment, an activist friar equally at
home on an assembly line or tramping in sandals along highways
and byways, but also a respectable burgher hungry for recognition and haunted by his failures in life. In hindsight, Étienne feels
his father must have spent at least ten years of his life in a deep
depression. At times, his eccentricities were hard to take—it wasn't
fun hanging out with friends and running into your father in a
jacket, tie, black shoes and socks, with his thin, hairy legs sticking
out of Adidas shorts—but he was the least egoistical of men and
his son cannot remember him ever behaving dishonorably. From
Mosaic law, he had adopted the commandment to give 10 percent
of his earnings to the poor, and if at the end of the year he hadn't
managed to set this sum aside, he borrowed it to fulfill his duty.

He was a just man, melancholy and disheartened, but a just man withal, against whom Étienne never had to rebel, and his own choices, he claims, carry on those of his father.

Although not a believer, Étienne follows the teachings of the Gospel and fondly remembers the chaplain of his school in Sceaux, just south of Paris, who championed the poetic writings of Dom Hélder Câmara and other liberation theologians. Étienne doesn't think it's an accident that three of his friends from those days became magistrates as well, men among the most brilliant and left-leaning of their generation. Like his father, in the end Étienne tried to change society, to make it more just, except that he tried to be shrewder than his old man, a reformer instead of a Don Quixote.

Later, Étienne told me something else about his father. I had gone to see him in August in the paternal family house in Corrèze, an edifice of thick stones with narrow doors and windows that has belonged to the Rigal family since the seventeenth century. His father was the one who insisted on buying the house from a cousin and restoring it with an authenticity precluding heating and other comforts, and it was he, with his wife, who assembled those peasant furnishings, the bread bins, dark wooden sideboards, and heavy cathedral chairs with hard backs that seem straight out of a painting by Le Nain but inspire no longing to sit in one to read by the fire. Étienne remembers with pleasure his summer vacations in the house, in fact he still goes back sometimes, but he's nevertheless convinced that his father was sexually abused there as a child. He has no evidence to back up this claim, which reminds me of an American biography of the novelist Philip K. Dick that makes the same assumption about its subject: though the author has no proof that the novelist was raped as a child, he feels that everything in Dick's personality points in that direction, to that trauma. When I mention this to Étienne, he sees the parallel and admits that his conviction has more to do with himself than with reality; perhaps his suspicion is unfounded, maybe it's only his imagination working up an explanation for his father's fear of physical contact. He was a loving father, God knows, and even better, a father who was able to instill confidence in his children, but he never kissed them, never took them in his arms, and even the slightest brush against them would make him shudder as if he'd touched a snake. So perhaps he wasn't raped, but there's no doubt the human body disturbed him deeply.

Did Étienne have this same problem? At first he said no, things were fine; then, on reflection, he said he'd been a solitary child at school, lost in daydreams, tormented by nightmares, and a bed wetter until he was sixteen. I'm familiar with those traits—although I did stop wetting my bed at an earlier age—and I can say that no, things weren't fine at all.

Early on, Étienne understood that he wanted to be a judge, a vocation that intrigues me. In high school I knew a boy who wanted to become a judge. I don't know if he became one, but as I recall he was a scary guy. He gave the impression that when he said judge he meant "cop," and a certain kind of cop: wily, suspicious, and perverse, a cop into whose hands you wouldn't want to fall. Perhaps I was mistaken, though; perhaps we were all mistaken, we young readers of *Charlie Hebdo*, the satiric political magazine. Maybe the scary boy was simply shy, proud of his intended vocation, wounded by our mockery, and perhaps he grew up to be as remarkable as Étienne Rigal. Maybe if I'd known Étienne Rigal back then, I would have been suspicious of him, too. I don't believe so; I'd rather think that we'd have become friends.

One of the things that made me want to write this story is the way Étienne said, The first time we met, Juliette and I, *we were great judges.* He spoke with unmistakable pride and confidence. He spoke as an artist who, while knowing that his career isn't over, that he must go on, keep striving, also knows that he has to his credit one accomplishment, at least, that will let him sleep easy come what may: he has made his mark. All the same, the idea of greatness applied to a judge perplexed me. Asked to name three great judges or even just one, I'd come up blank. Even though we may all subscribe to the conventional—and fair—idea that what matters isn't what you do but how you do it and that it's better to be a good butcher than a bad painter, we still generally make a distinction between creative professions and all the rest, and it's the creative ones that usually inspire us to see excellence (defined not only as competence but as talent and charisma, too) in terms of greatness. Regarding the legal profession: a great lawyer, I could see what that meant; a great bailiff, not really. And a great judge, frankly, especially when we're talking about a *juge d'instance,* a specialist not in major criminal cases but in civil disputes over property lines, trusteeships, unpaid rent—let's just say I didn't find the idea all that inspiring.

(And then there's the Gospel according to Matthew: "Judge not . . .")

To explain his vocation, Étienne says three things. That he loved the idea not of defending the widow and the orphan but of saying what is right and dispensing justice. That he wanted to change society, sure, but also to live a bourgeois life, a comfortable life, free of financial worries. And finally, that judges exercise power and that he has, if not a taste for power, then some taste for power.

When he said that he hadn't a taste for power but *some* taste for it, I didn't really get the nuance, but it illustrates a characteristic I like and have learned to recognize in Étienne. Even on the day of the family visit, I noticed it. Every time someone interrupted Étienne, not to contradict him but to confirm, complete, or comment on something he'd said, he would shake his head and murmur that no, that wasn't quite it. Then he'd continue, saying *almost*, but not *exactly*, the same thing. Thinking a little along his lines, I believe he needs to disagree with people in order to agree with them. For example, when Juliette's father mentioned Étienne's friendship with Juliette, Étienne picked up on that word: Juliette and he were not friends, they were close, and that wasn't the same thing at all. When I knew him better, I told him that to me *friendship* seemed like the right word for what existed between him and Juliette and if that wasn't it then I didn't see what friendship could be. While remaining alert to his obvious fondness for precision, I began teasing him about his mania for quibbling over whatever people said to him by saying almost the same thing back, and it amused him to be teased about that. We're always pleased when people who love us pounce on our shortcomings as extra reasons to love us. From then on, he consented more and more often to agree with me.

11

—

It's January 1981. I'm twenty-three, fulfilling my military obligation with alternative service in Indonesia, where I'm writing my first novel. Étienne is eighteen, in his last year of high school in Sceaux. He knows what he wants to do next: law school, then l'École nationale de la Magistrature (ENM), the nation's school for the training of judges and prosecutors. Étienne plays tennis. He's still a virgin. And for several months now, his left leg has been hurting. A lot. And more and more. After a few inconclusive consultations, there's a biopsy; when the results are in, his father immediately drives Étienne to the Institut Curie in Paris. His face is solemn, distressed; he doesn't use the fateful word but tells his son through gritted teeth that there are suspicious cells. In a basement room, several doctors are gathered around the boy. Well, young man, says one, we'll try to keep you whole.

You won't be going home. You're staying here.

What's going on?

You didn't understand? exclaims his father, upset and sorry that he'd been too vague. You have cancer.

Visitors and family members must leave at eight. Étienne is alone in his hospital room. He's had dinner, a pill to help him sleep; soon the light is turned off. It's nighttime. The first night, the one he spoke about the day we met. And this time he tries, because it's important, so important, to tell me everything.

He's lying in bed in his underpants; his father hadn't thought that events would move so swiftly, that his son would be staying in the hospital, and he hadn't brought any overnight things. Étienne lifts the blanket to look at his legs, his two legs that seem normal, an athletic teenager's legs. In the left one, in the left tibia, there's *that*, working to destroy it.

A couple of months earlier, he'd read Orwell's *1984*. One scene had particularly unnerved him. Winston Smith, the hero, is in the hands of the political police, and the officer interrogating him explains that his job is to find, for each suspect, the thing that scares him the most. People can be tortured, have their nails or testicles torn away, but some victims won't give in, you can't identify them in advance, and the heroes aren't always the ones you might think. Once you've identified a man's deepest fear, however, you've won. Heroism isn't possible anymore, no resistance is: when you can bring in his wife and child and ask if he'd rather have *that* done to him or to them, then no matter how brave he is and even if he loves his wife and child more than himself, he'll say, Them. That's how it is. There are horrors, different for each of us, that we cannot face. As for Smith, the officer has investigated and discovered that in his case the appalling, unbearable

thing is a caged rat held up close to his face, a famished rat that
leaps through the opened door to devour him, its sharp teeth biting his cheeks, nose, soon finding the choicest morsels, the eyes,
and tearing them out.

That's the image that comes to Étienne on his first night. *But
this rat is inside him.* Eating him alive. Starting with his tibia, then
moving up the leg; soon it will be cutting a path through his gut,
along his spine, right into his brain. And the rat is an image more
than a sensation; strangely, Étienne doesn't feel a thing, as if his
body and the relentless pain tormenting him for months had
gone, but the image is so unbearable that he wishes he could die
to break free of it, because he'd rather the light in his brain went
out and everything stopped and he himself just disappeared—if
that would get rid of the rat. Trapped in his horror, Étienne manages to tell himself that he has only one way out: he must find
something else. A different image . . . other words . . . If only he can
get through the night, something will happen. Maybe it won't save
him, but it will release him from *that.* Thanks to the sleeping pill,
he half dozes, while the rat gnaws and prowls. Étienne goes to
sleep. Wakes up to sheets drenched with sweat. And at dawn, the
rat is gone. For good. In its place, a sentence has appeared, which
he can see as if it were written on the wall right before his eyes.

Étienne does not reveal this dazzling sentence. He produces
others I take for approximations, paraphrases, displaying none of
the force and clarity he ascribes to the one that came to him that
night. I record in my notebook: The cancerous cells are you, just
like the healthy ones. You *are* these cancer cells. They aren't a
foreign body, a rat that's gotten inside you. They're part of you.
You can't hate your cancer, because you can't hate yourself. (I think,
without saying out loud: Of course you can.) Your cancer isn't an
adversary, it's you: *il est toi.*

I understand what Étienne is telling me: that these phrases

and the one still hidden behind them were decisive. I believe this, I know he's evoking something that rang absolutely true to him, but for the moment, I can't understand what he experienced. Just wait, I think; we're not finished with the first night . . .

The image of the rat, however, is familiar. Except that the animal gnawing away inside me is a fox. Étienne's rat is from *1984*; my fox is from the story of the little Spartan boy I read in Latin class. The boy had stolen a fox he kept hidden beneath his tunic, but as he stood in the Assembly of the Elders, the fox began to bite his belly. Rather than free the animal and reveal his theft, the boy let it eat into his stomach, without flinching, until he died.

I told Étienne that I had once gone to see the elderly psycho-analyst François Roustang. I spoke to him about the fox, which I still hoped to chase away by discovering how and why, toward the end of my childhood, it had lodged itself under my sternum to compress and chew on my solar plexus. Roustang shrugged. He no longer believed in explanations or even in psychoanalysis, only in rightness of action. Let it out, he said. Let it curl up there, on the couch. That's all you can do. You see, there it is. Lying quietly. And when I left, as he shook my hand, he added, You can leave it with me, if you like. I'll take care of it for you.

For a while I thought that would work. I didn't return to fetch the fox; it came back on its own. These days it leaves me alone, because it has either fallen asleep or gone away (I hope) forever, but at the time of my conversations with Étienne, it was still mak-ing me suffer. And it helped me to listen to what he had to say.

They began chemotherapy right away in an effort to save his leg, and save it they did. Étienne bravely endured most of the treatment, but what he couldn't bear was the idea of losing his hair. He was an edgy teenager, tormented, his virility still in flux. He found girls as frightening as they were attractive. So when his hair began to fall out, when his reflection in the mirror began to morph into a bald zombie without eyebrows or pubic hair, all those assurances that everything would grow back quickly meant nothing, the anguish was too strong, and he stopped the treatments. Secretly, on his own, without telling anyone. He had just a few half-day appointments left to go, not the full three-day sessions he'd had at the beginning. Although his parents offered to drive him, he said he preferred to take the métro, but then he didn't. At the Institut Curie, he explained that he was continuing his treatment at a clinic in Sceaux; he even asked them for a prescription, and he must have been convincing because no one called his parents to check that the protocol was being properly followed. He spent these free hours wandering around Paris, browsing in the bookstores of the Latin Quarter. What was going through his mind as he cut his chemo the way one cuts useless classes at the end of the year? Was he aware of the risk he was taking? He says yes. He also says that when he relapsed he wondered, If I'd stuck with the chemo to the end, would I have gotten sick again? Would they have cut off my leg? He still has no answer and says he quickly lost interest in the question.

He passed his baccalaureate exam in June and that summer, rather than rest as he'd been advised to do, he found a job at a sporting goods store, at the tennis racket counter. He was forbidden to play tennis because if his tibia broke it wouldn't heal, which didn't stop him from playing tennis and even soccer, a sport with the maximum risk of getting kicked, with spikes no less, and right in the tibia. Whether he was showing the normal bravado of an adolescent who's had a brush with death and wants to live on his own terms or whether there was a darker impulse at work here—that's another question he doesn't answer.

After a year, he was pronounced cured. He needed simply to have checkup exams every three months, then every six. He would go to the Institut straight from his law courses at the Panthéon. When he went in for his checkups, he'd look at the cancer patients in the waiting room with real disgust. One day, he remembers, they brought a woman in on a stretcher who must have weighed less than eighty pounds, with a face as wrinkled as a shrunken head. She was seen immediately and Étienne thought angrily, Why does she get to go ahead of me when I have so much to do in life, while all she's got left is to die? He wasn't ashamed of this harsh attitude—on the contrary, it fed his pride. Sickness revolted him, sick people did too, and all that had nothing to do with him anymore.

12

―

He was twenty-two when it came back. His leg ached, the same one, hurt so much he couldn't sleep and walked only with difficulty. I find it hard to believe when he assures me neither he nor his parents immediately feared a relapse, but, well, they were so convinced he'd been cured they thought a pain in his leg, even a bad one, couldn't be anything more serious than a pulled muscle or tendinitis. He did not, in any case, *recognize* the pain. But back he went to the Institut Curie for his X-ray and this time the results—when he returned for them three days later—were clear: the words *cancer* and *amputation* said everything.

The medical meeting with the medical team was at one o'clock and that morning at nine, at the Panthéon, he was to take his oral exam for his master's degree. The examiner was late; he had still not arrived by eleven. Étienne went to the secretary's office to explain his situation, that he had to be at the Institut Curie at one. It was important: they were going to decide whether or not to cut off his leg. Étienne has nothing against theatrics and relished the secretary's sudden discomfiture. She suggested, given the circumstances, that he receive special dispensation to postpone the exam, but he nixed that, so she scrambled to find another examiner. Étienne feels that he did well on his oral and, considering both his qualifications and the compassion his predicament should have inspired, he's still surprised that he received only a low-average grade.

At the Institut, the verdict was definitive: cancer of the fibula, amputation as soon as possible. As they had four years earlier, the doctors wanted to hospitalize him immediately so they could operate the next day, but Étienne was insistent: there was a party the following Sunday for his girlfriend's twentieth birthday and he intended to go. It was agreed that he would return to the hospital Sunday evening to be operated on the following morning.

I try to imagine not only his state after the consultation but that of his father, who had accompanied him. There's a worse nightmare than learning your leg will be cut off: it's to learn that your twenty-two-year-old son is going to lose his leg. What's more, his father had suffered in his youth from osteal tuberculosis, so he wondered if Étienne's cancer could be somehow connected to that, and this highly unlikely hypothesis added guilt to his already appalling feeling of helplessness. Distraught, he began talking seriously about having his own leg amputated to replace his son's lost limb. Étienne laughed and said, Don't want your old leg, you keep it.

He asked his father to drive him to the home of Aurélie—his girlfriend, who also lived in Sceaux—and pick him up later. He'd been with Aurélie for two years; they'd had their first sexual experiences with each other. She was very pretty, slender, and even now he thinks they might well have gotten married one day. They lay down on her bed; he said to her, Monday they're going to cut my leg off, and he finally began to cry. As night fell, they lay in each other's arms for hours, or rather, he lay in hers as she held him as tight as she could, caressing his hair, his face, his whole body, perhaps even the leg that would soon be gone. She whispered tender words to him, but when he asked her if she would still love him with only one leg, she was honest. She replied, I don't know.

A strange thing happened the night before the party. Without telling his father where he was going, Étienne borrowed the family car and drove into Paris, to a sauna on the rue Sainte-Anne, to have sex with a guy. He had never done that before, never did it again, he doesn't feel at all homosexual but that evening he did it. It was one of the last things he did with his two legs. Did what, exactly? As in certain dream experiences, he doesn't remember any of it, or yes, some peripheral details. The drive to Paris. Parking the car in a lot on the avenue de l'Opéra, then looking for that street where he'd never been before, paying the entrance fee, undressing, stepping naked into the steam room where other naked men were tentatively brushing up against one another, sucking one another off, taking one another up the ass. Did he suck anyone off, was he sucked off? Did he take anyone up the ass, was he taken? What did the guy look like? All that, the heart of the scene, is gone from his memory. He knows only that it happened. Then he drove back to Sceaux, found his parents still awake, and talked to them, in that neutral tone you use when there's been a catastrophe and there is nothing, in fact, you can say about it.

* * *

I don't know if the preceding paragraph will appear in the book. Étienne was clear on this point: Everything I tell you, he said, you can write down, I don't want to exert any control. Still, I'd understand perfectly if, while reading the text before publication, he were to ask me to keep quiet about that episode. Out of concern for those he loves rather than shame, because I'm sure he's not ashamed: it's a strange thing to have done, one he can't fully explain to himself, but it isn't a bad thing. Anyway, even a bad action—I don't think he'd be ashamed of that, either. Or he would, but he'd consider the shame a good thing to mention as well. He'd simply say: I did it, I'm ashamed of it, that shame is part of me, I will not deny it. The dictum "I am a man and nothing human is alien to me" strikes me as the last word in wisdom, or at least close to it, and what I love in Étienne is that he takes it literally. In my opinion that's what gives him the right to be a judge. He doesn't want to edit out anything that makes him human, uncertain, fallible, magnificent, and that's also why, in this account of his life, I don't want to cut anything either.

(Étienne's note, in the margin of the manuscript: "No problem, keep it.")

Aurélie's birthday celebration was not a party just for young people. Her friends were there, but also her parents and her parents' friends, all ages mixed together. It was an afternoon affair, in a garden full of flowers. A show had been rehearsed; Étienne was to sing. He sang. The pain was such that he had to lean on crutches. Everyone there knew he was going into the hospital that very evening to have his leg amputated in the morning.

At around six o'clock, he was lying beneath a tree, his head on Aurélie's lap, while she stroked his hair. Sometimes he looked up at her face. She'd smile at him, saying softly, I'm here, Étienne.

I'm here. He'd close his eyes again. He'd had something to drink, not much; he was listening to the murmur of conversation around them, the buzzing of a wasp, the car doors slamming in the street. He felt good and would have liked that moment to go on forever, or for death to take him like that, without his even knowing. Then his father came to get him and said, Étienne, it's time to go. Today he still thinks about what it meant for his father to have to say, Étienne, it's time to go. It seems an impossible thing to do and yet he did it. Those words were said, those actions taken calmly, but after all, Étienne says, there was nothing else to do. Except, yes, actually: he could have begun screaming, struggling, yelling *No, I don't want to!* Like certain people condemned to death and waiting in their cells when they hear those same words: It's time to go. But no, people helped him get up, and he got up.

That's it: I'm getting up to go get my leg cut off.

13

He'd asked those he loved to be there when he woke up and they are, all there around him: his parents, his brother, his sisters, and Aurélie. The first sensation as he emerges from the anesthesia is that it doesn't hurt anymore. The tumor had been compressing a nerve, causing pain that for the last several months had been excruciating. So he's no longer in pain; he feels nothing. But he sees: the shape of his right leg stretched out under the sheet, the shape of his left thigh, and just where there ought to be a knee the sheet collapses, there's nothing more. It will take some time before he dares raise the sheet and blanket, before he sits up to hold out his hand, moving it back and forth in the space where his leg used to be. He has one less leg, that's all he thinks about— and at the same time he keeps forgetting that. If he doesn't look at the empty spot that has replaced his leg, if he doesn't verify that it's no longer there, there's nothing to remind him that it's gone. His rational brain has registered the information, but it isn't his rational brain that is conscious of his body and makes it move. When the day comes for him to get dressed, to put on his boxer shorts, he won't be at a loss, he'll have prepared for this, thinking: I've had an amputation and will now perform a certain action for the first time since my operation and I'll have to do it differently this time. He will have thought this, yet when he holds out his boxers with both hands and bends over, he will first make as if to put his left foot through the left opening, knowing perfectly well, seeing perfectly clearly, that he no longer has a left foot, and he'll have to make a conscious effort to put only his right foot through the right opening, and slowly draw the boxers up his right leg and the column of emptiness on the other side, until the left opening slips over the absent knee and he can continue as he always has up along his thighs and finally over his buttocks and voilà: he has put on his underpants. It will be like this with everything. He'll have to adjust the program, shifting from business as usual to amputee mode. He'll have to domesticate not only the void replacing the leg but also the place where the void and the truncated leg meet, which has a terrible name and designates something not too pleasant, either: the stump. There is another crucial moment in the apprenticeship, when the hand, for the first time, touches the stump. It's not far away, just reach out . . . but *touching* it will inspire a certain revulsion and Étienne will need a long time yet—he's nowhere near that stage—before he can envisage the possibility that his stump won't always be a forbidden zone and that another person, in particular a woman, could one day touch and even caress that stump with love. All this education awaits him at the rehabilitation facility in Valenton, near Créteil, where the hospital has transferred him. Étienne passes quickly over this part of the story. What he does say is that a lot of lies get told about an amputation. They'll tell you, The amputation will be just above the knee, the ideal height for the prosthesis, and soon you'll be living a normal life. Then you get to the rehab center and ask the doctor when you can start playing tennis again and he looks at you as if you were nuts. Ping-Pong, sure, Ping-Pong's fine, but tennis, forget it. And you'll get told as well that once you're used to the prosthesis it will be a part of you, as if you actually had a new leg. Then the day comes when you try it on; the thing goes click-clack . . . and you see what a farce this is, it'll never be a new leg. Watching you cry, the caregivers tell you gently that everyone goes through this, that's why the apprenticeship takes time, but the other amputees, the ones a little ahead of you in that department, will tell you, as at least one of them told him, Welcome to the club. From now on you're one of us, three-quarters human with metal for the rest.

Étienne ran away. He was supposed to stay in rehab for three months, but the week he started he asked his parents to buy him a car, his first car—for the disabled (with one floor pedal)—so he could leave whenever he wanted, and after two weeks he'd gone home. Like the cancer patients at the Institut, the amputees at Valenton disgusted him. He wanted nothing to do with any friendship or even camaraderie nourished by *that* solidarity.

The year of chemotherapy, on the other hand, was nonnegotiable. It was atrocious. Three all-day sessions once a month, and during those three days, bluntly put, you never stop vomiting. Three days of throwing up when you've got nothing left to throw up. Each month, the idea of going back through all that again terrified him. As a rule, he thinks one must live lucidly, experiencing everything that happens, even suffering; that was already his credo, even then, but *that*—no, that served no purpose, was too disgusting, too humiliating, it was better to be unconscious, and he asked for the oblivion of drugs. He allowed his mother to come hold the basin for him, but not Aurélie; he didn't want her to see him like that. Now, twenty years later, he's sorry. He says it's one of the real regrets of his life, much more lasting than having cut short his first round of chemotherapy. Aurélie wanted to be with him, she loved him and her place was at his side, but he hadn't let her be there. He hadn't trusted her.

Besides making him horrifically sick, the chemo made him lose all the hair on his body, just as he'd feared the first time. Almost all, but not quite; Aurélie had insisted that he shave what remained, but he refused, keeping a few long scraggles of hair that made him look even more hideous. Not without reason, Aurélie accused him of overdoing it. He'd stand looking at himself in the mirror: that white, scrawny, glabrous thing without a leg—that was him; the athletic young man of a just few months earlier was now this mutant. Aurélie hung on for almost a year before she left him. He was twenty-two. He was twenty-eight before he had another girlfriend.

After his first cancer, he'd gone to a psychotherapist. This had nothing to do with his illness, he says; at the time he'd thought himself cured. Sexual problems had prompted the therapy, and that's all he'll say on that topic, but what seems clear to me is that his present sexual confidence is a hard-won victory over years of misery. During the second cancer and the amputation, his psychotherapist came to the hospital every day. The man was barely ten years older than Étienne, and a patient that young, with cancer, and now an amputee . . . that was a first for him. We're both venturing into uncharted waters, he said: I don't know what to do or where we're heading. Étienne found that reassuring.

The psychotherapy turned into an analysis that lasted nine years. Throughout that period, during which Étienne attended the ENM in Bordeaux and worked as a judge in the north of France, he would take the train to Paris twice a week and never missed a session. This intense experience has given him, even more than familiarity with the unconscious, an almost religious confidence in its powers. He is not—or at least he says he's not—a believer, but he has a liking and a gift for abandoning himself to this force that, deep within him, is more powerful than he, and perhaps wiser as well. This force is not outside him; it is neither a personal nor a transcendent god. It's everything that while being him is not him, is beyond him, inspires him, gives him a rough time, saves him, and he has gradually learned to let it be. I wouldn't say that what he calls the unconscious is what Christians call God; perhaps it's what the Chinese call Tao.

At this point, I'm walking on eggshells. I suppose Étienne talked a lot about his cancer in analysis, and frankly I'm amazed that with his deep faith in the power of the unconscious he should refuse all psychosomatic interpretations of his disease. On this subject, though, he won't argue, he shoots on sight. He tells me, People who say that it starts in your head, comes from stress or some unresolved psychic conflict—I feel like killing them, and I feel like killing them all over again when they trot out the other cliché: You survived because you fought back, you have courage. That's not true. Some people fight back and they're incredibly courageous and they don't make it. Example: Juliette.

Étienne said that to us the day Juliette's family and I went to visit him; he said it again at my first private meeting with him, and both times I indicated that I agreed, but I'm not really sure I do. Of course, I have no theory of my own or any authority to have one on such a controversial question, and I'm aware that my opinions here say nothing about the etiology of cancer but reveal instead, at best, some things about myself. First, my gut feeling is that cancer is not a disease that hits you from outside, by accident (not always, anyway, and not necessarily). And more importantly, I'm convinced that deep down Étienne feels the same way—or that he rages so vehemently against this interpretation precisely because he fears it might be true.

In 1976 a book called *Mars*, by Fritz Zorn, was published. It made a considerable impression at the time, and I've since reread it. Here is how it begins:

"I am young, rich, and educated, and I'm unhappy, neurotic, and alone . . . My upbringing has been middle-class, and my life has been a model of good behavior. Naturally, I also have cancer, which goes without saying if you consider what I just told you." To Zorn, cancer is both a "disease of the body" that will quite probably soon kill him, although he might also defeat it and survive, and "a disease of the soul," about which he says simply: "I'm lucky it finally made its move."

The book's final sentence: "I declare that I am in a state of total war."

This may seem just too good to be true, but Zorn, which means "anger" in German, is a pseudonym for the author's real name, which is . . . Angst. In the course of his book, in his passage from anguish to anger, this docile, alienated young patrician, "educated to death," as he puts it, has become at once a rebel and a free man. His illness and the terrifying approach of death have taught him who he is, and to know who one is—Étienne would say, where one is—means the end of neurosis. Rereading *Mars*, I could not stop thinking about the life Fritz Zorn would have had if he'd survived, about the accomplished man he might have become if he'd been granted the chance to enjoy that expansion of consciousness for which he paid so dearly. And I thought that Étienne was a man who had accomplished that very feat.

I didn't dare tell him that or bring up another book that had impressed me almost as much as *Mars*. *Le Livre de Pierre* is a long interview by Louise Lambrichs with Pierre Cazenave, a psychoanalyst who suffered from cancer for fifteen years and died of it before the book came out. He described himself not as "having cancer" but as "being cancerous." "When I learned of my cancer," he says, it seemed "that I had always had it. It was my identity." Psychoanalyst and "cancerous," he became a psychoanalyst for "the cancerous," grounding his approach in his intuitive understanding that "the worst suffering is the one you cannot share. And a cancer patient usually feels that suffering twice over. Because he cannot share the anguish of sickness with those around him and because beneath this pain lies another, more ancient one, dating back to childhood, and it, too, has never been shared, never been seen. And that is the worst of fates: never to have been seen, never to have been acknowledged."

This other suffering, says Cazenave, is what he aspires to cure, by leading his patients to see and recognize it for what it is and thereby escape its torment. His patients will still die, but between Molière, who mocked doctors who "cured" their victims to death, and the great English psychoanalyst D. W. Winnicott, who asked God for the blessing of dying completely alive, Cazenave clearly sides with Winnicott. Cazenave focuses on people who approach their cancer not as the random visitation of catastrophe but as a truth that concerns them intimately, an obscure consequence of their own history, the ultimate expression of their unhappiness and dismay as they deal with life.

Cazenave is speaking of himself as well when he says that in such patients something has gone wrong during the developmental stage of primary narcissism, leaving a profound flaw in the oldest core of the personality.* This means, he says, that there are two kinds of people: those thus damaged, who often dream about falling into a void, and everyone else—all those who have been well supported by a "holding environment" and can thus stand and live confidently on solid ground. The damaged ones, though, will suffer all their lives from vertigo and anguish, from a sense of not really existing. This infantile malformation may persist a long time in the adult as a kind of background noise, a depression—unrecognized even by its victim—that will one day become malignant. Such patients, informed they have cancer, are not surprised, for they somehow recognize the malignancy, knowing that it was *themselves*. All their lives, they have feared something that has in fact already happened. Cazenave believes that in patients damaged by this childhood malformation of the self (and who have of course forgotten it), the memory of the wound awakens at the news of their mortal illness, as the fresh disaster reactivates the old one, causing an intolerable psychic distress whose specific origin they do not yet fully understand.

In that panic and distress Cazenave sees the desperate flailing of a deeply flawed creature that never really felt it had a right to live and now suddenly hears its days are numbered. For someone who has always felt alive, a death sentence is sad, cruel, unfair, but it can be integrated into the order of things. But for someone who deep inside has always had the sense of not truly *being*? Of never having lived? For that person, Cazenave holds out the promise of transforming illness and even the approach of death

---

* Freud describes the infant's initial focus on the self, a kind of self-love the child is unable to separate from sexual desire, as "primary" or "normal" narcissism, a healthy defense mechanism that shields the child's psyche during the formation of the individual self.

into one last chance to be really present in this world. He quotes Céline's wrenching, mysterious words: "Maybe that's what we seek our whole lives long, nothing more: the greatest possible sorrow, so that we can become ourselves before we die." Pierre Cazenave is not a theoretician, he speaks only from experience, his own and that of his patients, to whom he is bound by "unconditional solidarity with what the human condition holds of unfathomable distress." (That is the formula with which he defines his art, and I would like to be worthy of claiming it for my own.)

In the clinical picture described by Cazenave, I recognize once again Jean-Claude Romand, who—it's horrible to say this—was not lucky enough to have cancer and so invented one for himself, because in some dark way he knew that malignancy was his truth and he longed to have his cells recognize this truth. Since they did not, his only recourse was to lie. I also recognize a part of myself, the part that recognized itself in Romand, but I was able to make books out of my "illness" instead of metastases or lies. And I recognize as well something of Étienne, who had awful nightmares, wet his bed for years, and is convinced his father was raped as a child.

Well, of course I don't believe this is *the* explanation for cancer, but I do believe that certain people have been damaged at their core almost from the beginning and cannot, despite their courage and best efforts, really live. I also believe that one of the ways in which life, which wants to live, works its way through such people can be in disease, and not just any disease: cancer. That's why I'm so stunned by people who claim that we are free, that happiness can be decided, that it's a moral choice. For these cheerleaders, sadness is in bad taste, depression a sign of laziness, melancholy a sin. Yes, it is a sin, even a mortal sin, but some people are born sinners, born damned, and all their courage and best efforts will not set them free. These people who are damaged at the core are as cut off from the rest of humanity as the poor are from the wealthy. It's like the class struggle: we know some of the poor will manage to escape their lot but most won't, and telling a melancholic that happiness is a decision is like telling a starving man simply to eat cake. So when Pierre Cazenave insists that mortal illness and death can offer such people a chance to live at last, I believe it, and all the more readily since at certain moments of my life, I must confess, I was wretched enough to long for that fate. As I write this, I think I have put those days behind me. I'll even venture to say, presumptuous though it may be, that I am cured. But I want to remember. I want to remember the person I was and the many others like me. I never want to be that person again—but I never want to forget him, either, or to despise the man being gnawed at by the fox and who began, three years ago, to write this account.

The Scorpion-Fish, the Nicolas Bouvier book I was reading in Sri Lanka, ends with another line from Céline: "The worst defeat in everything is to forget, and especially what did you in."

14

—

After finishing the ENM, Étienne made two choices: to join the left-wing Syndicat de la Magistrature, a public and active union of judges, and to take a difficult position as a sentencing judge in Béthune, a city at the tip of northern France.* The Syndicat was widely seen as a haven for lefty judges who refused to join the elite, enjoyed chasing after white-collar criminals, and raised hackles by dispensing their own form of class justice. The classic example of that last tendency was the brief imprisonment of an unpopular notary in Bruay-en-Artois accused of rape and murder not because of convincing evidence but because he had a fine house, a fine car, and a bourgeois potbelly. As for Béthune, it's

---

* In the French criminal justice system, sentencing judges are responsible for both imposing and carrying out sentences as well as deciding on parole and postincarceration monitoring.

just like Bruay, in fact: the dilapidated North, with unemployment, poverty, abandoned slag heaps, parking-garage rapes of illiterate alcoholics by other illiterate alcoholics.

Étienne's two choices seemed like a good match, but they eventually placed him in a difficult position. Under Mitterrand, the Syndicat had managed to acquire some real clout in political circles. Its elder members, veterans of '68 now in their forties who had hitched themselves to the left's rising star, had commandeered important judicial positions. They could look forward to a good twenty more years in which to monopolize their cushy posts and block the careers of younger colleagues, but they didn't mind throwing a few crumbs to a talented and accommodating beginner like Étienne. The young hope of the judicial left, Étienne was tapped for a commission on sentencing reform that might conceivably have paved his way to a ministerial position. It was a tempting offer. By his own admission, Étienne's desire to be a judge reflected a taste for power and comfortable living, and he could hardly ignore the fact—with his acute class consciousness—that his chosen profession was losing status in the world. Judges had once had considerable standing, but in 1989, for example, the year he left the ENM, a downgrade in protocol left them ranked below subprefects, and their invitations to official receptions began to dry up. Unlike most high-ranking civil servants, whose jobs come with lodgings and an official car (especially in the provinces), judges had lost their previous perks. They worked in poorly heated premises with old rotary phones, no computers, and surly secretaries. In one generation, the leading citizen who lorded it over others became an ordinary man who traveled by métro, ate his lunch off a cafeteria tray, and more and more often this ordinary man was a woman—an infallible sign of the proletarianization of a profession. Étienne had every reason to grab the first chance he could to migrate upward to classier spheres. Just how strongly the commission offer was put to him he doesn't say, but I know he's too proud a man to boast and I believe it was again his pride that led him to choose, really choose to stay on as a low-level judge among the down-and-out in that grim city in the North.

What Étienne does in his office as a sentencing judge is something like what a psychoanalyst does in his. His role is to listen and find out what the person in front of him is able to understand.

The walking wounded are his clientele: many are heroin addicts and HIV positive. Their chances of making it are not good, so words of encouragement are in theory useless. Yet a judge can offer them anyway, words that are both true and timely, and sometimes even helpful.

Faced with these lost souls, so beaten down, doomed from the start, Étienne discovers that the more painful their stories are, the calmer he is. Listening to the sufferings of others, he instinctively adopts the attitude that guided him through his ordeal with cancer, anchoring himself in a core of strength. No revolt, no struggle; let things—the drug, the illness, life itself—run their course. Now, too, he doesn't hunt for the perfect thing to say; just lets the words come on their own. They may not be the right ones, but this is the only way the right ones have a chance of coming.

Often, he talks about himself. To those who are afraid and despise themselves, he speaks of his own fear, of the degraded self-image he'd once had. To the sick, he speaks of his illness. He doesn't mince words. His two cancers and missing leg impress the people who come before the bench, he knows that. He uses such experiences shamelessly, happy to find they serve a purpose.

What purpose, exactly? Being more human? Wiser? Better?

Étienne says he hates that idea. I tell him it seems right to me.
The orthodox view, Hélène might say, a little RC, but still, *right*,
and he's the living proof of that.

Meaning what? I'm a nice guy because I had cancer and got a
leg cut off? You're serious?

No, no, I say. It's more complicated than that, I agree: a guy
can have had cancer and still be a shit or an imbecile, but in fact
yes, that is what I mean. What I don't say, just as I don't talk about
Fritz Zorn or Pierre Cazenave, is that I think his cancer cured
him of what ailed him.

I try to imagine him, this young judge hobbling along the side-
walks of Béthune. He doesn't live there, he needn't go *that* far;
he's got an apartment in Lille, full of books and records. In the
evening, he takes off his prosthesis and goes to bed. Alone, always
alone. The medical treatments, the physical damage, the loss of
his hair have put his libido through the wringer. He's doing better now, his hair has grown back, he's got some pep; you could say
he's an attractive man, but you can't honestly say that it's not a
problem in life and with women to be missing a leg. The woman
who will accept him as he is, the one who would have loved him
with two legs but will meet and love him with only one—he
doesn't know her yet. Does he believe she will come, that something will shift, bringing love, confidence, and trust within reach?
Or does he despair? No, he doesn't despair. Even at the worst of
times, he never truly loses hope. He has always kept the elementary appetite for life that made him go straight from his hellish
chemo sessions at the Institut Curie to the café across the street,
where he would belly up to the counter and order a huge sausage
sandwich and tear into it while thinking, It's still good to be alive,
still good to be Étienne Rigal. Nevertheless, he is caught in what

psychiatrists call a double bind, a twofold constraint that makes him lose on both counts. Heads I win, tails you lose. To be rejected because he's got only one leg, that's hard; to be desired for the same reason, that's worse. The first time a girl let me know she didn't want to sleep with me because of my leg, he says, it was a slap in the face. But I once heard another girl say in front of a whole bunch of people, Sleeping with Étienne would really excite me because of his wooden leg. Well, that was even harder to take, I mean it. But you have to learn to take that, too. One thing that helped me: toward the end of this long sexual drought, I had a relationship with a girl who'd been raped as a child by her father and later, as a teenager, by two strangers. She was completely terrorized by sex. I was too, at the time. So we were both terrorized, which is probably why we wound up in bed together. We did what we could to be less afraid—and it was incredible. Sexually incredible, I mean it, with fantastic tenderness and abandon, one of the great experiences of my life. When women, or boys, who've been raped come before me in court, I sometimes tell them about this liberating relationship. Then I tell them, It's real, what happened to you; it's an awful trauma, a handicap that hurts your sexuality, but you need to know that there are good people out there who will deal just fine with your handicap, and if you accept this, you'll be fine, too.

When I Googled "sexuality" and "handicap," I found a site called OverGround pitched at people sexually attracted to amputees. They call themselves devotees, and some are more than that, they're wannabes who'd like to be amputees themselves so they can identify with the objects of their desire. Wannabes who actually go through with amputations are rare; most just play with the idea, Photoshop their images so they can see what they'd look like

with the stump of their dreams. Those who go all the way live a
Calvary. I read one person's account of trying for years to find an
understanding surgeon who would cut off a healthy leg; in the
end he mutilated his own leg so badly with a hunting rifle that
amputation was inevitable. Devotees and wannabes form a shameful community that would like to throw off its shame. We're not
perverts, they say; our desires may be distinctive, unusual, but
they're natural and we'd like to be open about them. These
desires, they admit, are difficult to satisfy. The ideal pair would
be a devotee who found a wannabe who'd get an amputation, and
both would enjoy their perfect match in perfect harmony. The
Internet is good for facilitating these types of encounters—
assuming they take place between consenting adults—even, as
happened a few years ago, matching a man who wanted to eat
someone with a man who consented (at least at the beginning) to
be eaten. But this ideal conjunction is rare. For one thing, the
wannabe's vocation tends to be more phantasmic than anything
else. And as for the devotee, what usually happens in reality, as
with closeted homosexuals, is that he—let's say he's a man—is
married to a woman who is completely unaware of his desires and
who would be appalled if she discovered them. The OverGround
site advises the devotee to make cautious approaches, to propose
erotic games involving crutches to his companion, but it's obvious
that a taste for amputation is less "acceptable" than an interest in
sodomy or urophilia and that the chances of converting anyone to
this paraphilia are slim indeed. By far the most promising path
for the devotee is to find an amputee. In theory, you might think
that amputees, whose infirmity repulses many people, would be
happy to meet those who actually find them attractive. The problem, which even a militant and proselytizing site like OverGround
must acknowledge, is that most involuntary amputees—meaning

most amputees—react as Étienne did when that girl said she'd like to sleep with him because of his wooden leg: they feel disgusted with such desires. So the devotee's only recourse is hypocrisy: when courting an amputee, the devotee must carefully hide all attraction to that handicap and make the amputee feel desired in spite of it.

It was my second visit; Étienne and I had been talking all morning. At noon he called his wife and invited her to join us at the Italian restaurant where he'd taken me the first time we'd talked. I'd only seen Nathalie briefly at Juliette's funeral and was slightly uneasy about how she might view the bizarre endeavor her husband and I had embarked on, but as soon as she sat down on the banquette next to him, blond, cheerful, confident, my worries were over. The situation seemed to amuse her. Since Étienne trusted me, so did she, and they clearly enjoyed telling me in stereo about what in their personal mythology they called Sadie Hawkins time—an expression I didn't understand, meaning the period during a dance or a party when girls get to take the initiative.

Autumn 1994. Étienne is finishing his analysis. Even though nothing has changed objectively, he feels that something has opened inside him, and now it's up to life to make a move. His analyst agrees, so they're both prepared for the session they have jointly decided will be the last. It's a disconcerting moment. Twice a week for nine years, you've told someone everything you don't tell anyone else, establishing a relationship unlike any other, until by mutual agreement the relationship comes to an end—and this end is the crowning achievement of the relationship. Yes, definitely, it's disconcerting. Leaving that last session, Étienne takes the train at the Gare du Nord for Lille, where later that afternoon he will be teaching his first class to a group of very young lawyers. Nathalie is among them, and they all repair to a café afterward to continue talking. Some of them adored Étienne, others loathed him. She adored him, thought him brilliant, original, an iconoclast. Moved by his gentle voice, she intuits a richness of experience behind his sense of humor, an intriguing mystery. She makes inquiries, learns where he lives and that he lives alone, walks around alone, and goes alone to a big chain store, Fnac, to buy books. She likes him more and more. She begins to think he might be interested in another young woman, but she's not worried, because the other girl's already engaged and anyway, even if *he* doesn't know it yet, she does: he is the man of her life. She invites him to a party; he doesn't show. The course is a short one, only a few classes, and it ends. So she goes to see him at the courthouse and explains that the students would really like at least one more class to round things out. It isn't true, but she'll enlist a dozen pals as extras for that supplementary session, held informally at Étienne's apartment. Afterward, the extras vanish; Nathalie lingers and invites him to the movies. The film they see, Kieslowski's *Red*, tells the story of a limping, misanthropic judge, played by Jean-Louis Trintignant, but they pay no attention to this coincidence because after ten minutes she kisses him. They wind up at his place; she stays the night. Étienne realizes that something enormous is happening to him and becomes frightened. He'd been planning to leave the next day for a week's vacation in Lyon, staying with a woman friend, and thinking to calm down, get some perspective, he leaves. During the one night he spends in Lyon he understands not only that he has fallen in love but that this love is trusting, shared, certain, and that he will build his whole life on it. He calls Nathalie in the morning: I'm coming back, do you want to meet me at my place? Do you want to live with me? She arrives with all her possessions, and they've been together ever since. But Étienne has something else to tell her, and it's not good. Though he hasn't checked for several years, not wanting to damage his morale any more, he's fairly sure the chemo has made him sterile. Nathalie admits this is a drawback, because she does want children, but instead of balking at the problem she starts looking for a solution. She buys a book by the biologist Jacques Testart, the "scientific father" of France's first test-tube baby, on the various methods of assisted reproduction. If none of them work, she tells Étienne, we'll adopt. But first, he has to take the test again. She decides, organizes; he follows, dazed with admiration. Everything that weighs so heavily on his life—his missing leg, his fears, his probable sterility—she takes it on, she'll cope with it. It's part of the deal and the deal suits her. She goes with him when he masturbates at the medical center, and when they return for the results the following week, the secretary tells Étienne the intern wants to see them personally, which makes them nervous, but when the intern opens the door to the waiting room she smiles to see them clutching each other on the black leatherette bench, holding hands, and I smile as well, eleven years later, looking at them sitting on the restaurant banquette. I've had lots of bad news to announce lately, says the intern, so I feel like giving some good news: you can have a child. As they leave, they say, Well, shall we? A month later, Nathalie is pregnant.

She is from the North and has had enough of it, and so has he. Besides, for some time now one of the other sentencing judges has been telling Étienne (with that sagacious air of someone who can see what's good for you even better than you can) that he's a natural for the *tribunal d'instance*.* This colleague is a much older man, right-wing, Catholic, a real old-fashioned magistrate. Although they don't agree on much, they respect each other, and since Étienne hasn't any definite inclination himself, he rather likes the idea of relying on someone else's opinion, the way one would trust to chance or the way I consult the sibylline guidance of the I Ching in similar straits. Étienne thinks it's good to make decisions, but you can also decide to just go with the flow, to accept advice or an offer simply because you feel like it. You can resolve not to hinder the course of life by obsessing over something as contingent as what you want. As it happened, he says, I didn't really see myself as a *juge d'instance*, but if M. Bussières saw me there so clearly, why not? Why not apply for that position opening up at the *tribunal d'instance* in Vienne? Vienne, that's right next door to Lyon: Nathalie can practice as a lawyer in Lyon, plus it'll be warmer there than in Béthune.

---

* The *tribunal d'instance* is the lowest rung in the civil area of the French legal system, something like our small claims court, a court of original jurisdiction for minor civil litigation in which proceedings are usually oral and litigants are not required to be represented by an attorney. Unlike judges in the U.S. legal system, French judges are not impartial referees between plaintiffs and defendants but are instead trained to actively investigate charges as well as render decisions. A *juge d'instance* thus must engage with all sorts of human misfortune, face-to-face with plaintiffs who are often angry, alone, impoverished, and at their wits' end. Ideally the judge has at least a passing familiarity with many aspects of modern life, since in theory the next case could deal with anything at all.

15

Vienne, the subprefecture of the *département* of Isère, is a city of thirty thousand inhabitants, with Gallo-Roman ruins, a quaint historic district, a promenade lined with cafés, and an annual jazz festival in July. In fact, Vienne is as bourgeois as Béthune is run-down. Prominent citizens, commercial and legal family dynasties, severe facades concealing inheritance battles waged in close quarters: perhaps it amused Étienne to find himself in this province right out of a Claude Chabrol film, especially since there was no question of actually living in Vienne, merely of going there three times a week, a half-hour drive from the Perrache neighborhood in Lyon where he and Nathalie found the apartment they're still in today. Yes, it did amuse him, and his reports from the legal front made Nathalie laugh, because the center of gravity in their life was elsewhere, in this handsome apartment they enjoyed decorating

and where their second child had just been born. Still, on his first
day presiding in court, when the lawyer arrived thirty minutes
late without apologizing, Étienne understood that a test of strength
had begun that he could not afford to lose. The lawyers at the bar
of Vienne had been there for twenty years, they would still be
there in twenty years, their parents were there before them, and
their children would be there after them, so when a new judge
walked in, their first concern was to make him understand that
they owned the house in which he was simply a tenant, and they
expected him to follow house rules. Étienne summoned the lawyer and said pleasantly, Today was the first time, so I did not
call you on it in court, but please don't try it again or there'll be
trouble.

It worked.

When he'd been a sentencing judge, his work had consisted of
meeting with people in his office. In jeans and a T-shirt, he listened to them, talked to them, and came up with concrete solutions to their problems, solutions that usually had nothing to do
with the law. His dealings with these people could go on for
years. Now he wore a judge's robe and sat on a dais, flanked by a
clerk and an usher, also in robes, who showed him a degree of
deference he found a little too formal. That same first day, there
was another hitch: leaving his chambers, he gallantly stepped
aside to let his female court clerk pass in front of him, which so
startled her that she stopped short, as rattled as if she'd feared he
was about to goose her, and he noticed afterward that she was
now careful to stay far behind him until he'd crossed the threshold. With slightly trembling hands, she'd pretend until the last
moment to tidy files on the table. Étienne smiled at all this solem-

nity, but he missed the personal relationships with ordinary people. The decisions he was making affected the lives of men and women he'd seen for five or ten minutes at most. He was working no longer with individuals but with dossiers. What's more, he had to move quickly. The case overload meant justice had to be dispensed mechanically (this offense calling for that penalty, this contractual flaw entailing that legal consequence) and quickly, all the more so because productivity—the number of decisions rendered—was a major prerequisite for a judge's advancement. It didn't bother Étienne to work quickly—indeed, he likes it—but he promised himself he would never do shoddy work and would treat each dossier as a unique and singular story calling for a carefully tailored legal solution.

That autumn, I went twice to Vienne to wander around the courthouse. It's a handsome seventeenth-century building that dominates a small square featuring the Roman temple of Augustus and Livia, the pride of the city. When I was not "in court," as I caught myself saying one day, I met with judges, clerks, and lawyers to whom Étienne had spoken on my behalf. I questioned them about what exactly a *juge d'instance* does, about the way in which Juliette and Étienne had done it, and they asked me about what exactly I was planning to do with all that. A pious homage to my late sister-in-law? A report on French justice? A diatribe about debt management? I didn't know what to tell them. I did feel they were touched to see a writer take an interest in the *tribunaux d'instance*, which don't intrigue many people, but they were also wary. Étienne's name wasn't opening doors as widely as I'd hoped. When I called (at his suggestion) the woman who'd replaced him when he later left his position, I told her I hoped to spend a week or two closely observing the court in session. She replied that an internship could not be set up just like that. I hadn't mentioned any internship and was simply being polite, informing her I would be attending sessions generally open to the public, but as often happens when one foolishly requests an authorization one doesn't need, I got a whole song and dance: she couldn't assume responsibility for such approval, I had to contact the president of the court of appeal. And why not the keeper of the seals? joked Étienne, using a title held by the French minister of justice, and not surprised at all. I realized that the shadow of her predecessor loomed large over the new mistress of the premises, who must have seen me in some way as his spy, an emissary from the emperor come to stir up ghosts amid the Restoration.

I wound up doing something like an internship anyway and confirmed what Étienne had said: that a *juge d'instance* is the judicial equivalent of a neighborhood doctor. Overdue rents, evictions, garnished salaries, guardianships for handicapped or elderly people, lawsuits involving less than ten thousand euros (anything above that belongs in the *tribunal de grande instance*, which occupies a more elegant part of the courthouse). Anyone frequenting the court of assizes or even the criminal court would admit that the civil matters handled by the *tribunal d'instance* are meager indeed. Everything is petty there: the wrongs, the stakes, the reparations. Most people there are poor, true, though their poverty hasn't yet slid into criminality. The judge is mired in daily life, with struggling people whose difficulties are both ordinary and insurmountable, people who don't even show up in court, as a rule, and neither does their lawyer because they don't have one, so the judge simply sends them the verdict via registered letter, which half the time they don't dare go get at the post office.

* * *

The daily fare of the sentencing judge in the North was the delinquency of seropositive drug addicts. For the civil magistrate in Vienne, it's disputes over expenditures and debt. Vienne, as I said, is a bourgeois city, and Isère is hardly the poorest of French *départements*, but in just a few weeks Étienne realized he was living in a world where people were collapsing beneath their debts with no way out. In civil courtrooms, a little matter of a party wall or water damage was even welcome because it provided a break from the monotonous procession of lending institutions— banks and specialized credit companies—hauling debtors into court.

Neither life nor his studies had prepared Étienne for this form of social misfortune. The only time one of his professors at the ENM had spoken of consumer protection law, it was with ironic disdain, as if it concerned idiots who signed contracts without reading them and whom only a popularity-seeking politician would try helping. The foundation of civil law, the textbooks say, is the contract. And the foundation of the contract is the free will and equality of the parties involved. No one should enter into a contract unwillingly; those who do must accept the consequences— then they'll be more careful the next time. Étienne hadn't needed eight years up in Béthune to learn that people are neither free nor equal, but he remained attached to the idea (otherwise he wouldn't have been a jurist) that contracts should be respected. Raised in a middle-class environment, he had never known financial hardship. He and Nathalie had a joint checking account, a savings passbook, life insurance, and had taken out a loan to buy their apartment (repaid via monthly automatic deductions), a loan large enough so they could always afford to take a vacation. All Étienne knew about revolving credit was that his Fnac card, he'd been told, allowed him to charge items and pay for them the following month, but he preferred to pay cash for his books and records, treating himself to a few more of them thanks to his bonus points. Sometimes, but rarely, since he didn't leave much of a paper trail, he would receive in the mail brochures from consumer credit companies. "Dip into your cash account whenever you like," said Sofinco. "Treat yourself today," offered Finaref. "Need money? Fast?" asked Cofidis. "Take advantage now," urged Cofinoga. Étienne just threw them away.

Now that he'd seen people who signed such offers passing through his courtroom, Étienne took a good look at those brochures. He discovered how easy it is to persuade the poor that, even though they're poor, they can buy themselves a washing machine, a car, a Nintendo console for the kids, or simply something to eat, and to persuade them that they'll be able to pay the money back later *and* that it won't cost them anything more than if they'd paid cash up front. Unlike the more regulated and less costly loans issued by traditional banks, these contracts are concluded in an instant: just sign at the bottom of the brochure, which is labeled a "preapproved offer." You can do the same thing at the cash register. The card you get is valid right away and automatically renewed; you withdraw what you want, when you want—which gives the agreeable impression of receiving free money, an impression the wording of the terms does nothing to dispel. Nothing is said about a loan, it's a "cash account"; credit isn't mentioned, only "ease of payment." Example: "You need three thousand euros? How does three thousand euros for one euro per month sound? Well, chère Madame, you're in luck, because as a loyal customer— of our store, of our mail-order department—you've been approved for an absolutely exceptional offer. As of today, you can request a credit reserve for up to 3,000 euros." The exorbitantly high cost of this loan appears in tiny print on the back of the offer, whether you notice it or not (mostly not), and anyway you sign because when you have no money this is the only way to buy what you need, or maybe even just want, because even when you're poor you want things, that's the tragedy. In a situation where banks would have the prudence to say no, the consumer credit companies always say yes; that's why bankers always obligingly send them any customers in the red. The agencies don't care if you're already deep in debt. They don't check anything: sign the offer, spend, that's all they ask. Everything's fine as long as you make your monthly payment, or rather, payments, because the nature of this kind of credit is to multiply, so you wind up with a dozen of these cards. The day inevitably comes when missed payments overwhelm you and the credit company takes you to court, demanding collection of the sums owed, plus the interest stipulated in the contract, plus the late fees also stipulated in the contract, and it adds up to much more than you'd ever imagined.

One trial, that year, garnered lots of attention. A couple was earning 2,600 euros a month, he as a construction worker, she as a health care aide. They tried to kill themselves and their five children because after twelve years of their living on credit, with six bank accounts, twenty-one revolving credit accounts, fifteen ATM cards, and debts of almost 250,000 euros, their creditors had turned on them. Reminder letters for payment had replaced the engaging offers, and since everyone was attacking them at once, it was impossible to play one loan against another or open a new account to buy some time. The jig was up. One last card, not yet refused, bought new clothes so the children would arrive properly dressed in the next world, which their father imagined with sinister candor as "the same, but without debts." The collective suicide failed; only one of the girls succumbed. In the court of assizes, the father got fifteen years and the mother ten. The affair upset the entire nation. It's a pathetic case, Étienne tells me, but not really a good example, because the Cartier family essentially used credit to live beyond their means. They bought a television and a game console for each child, top-of-the-line appliances; they kept buying new cars, new furniture, new appliances; they signed up for and subscribed to everything—in short, they were obviously suckers for any salesperson who walked through the door. Sociologists call such people "active" compulsive debtors, and the hard times brought on by the recent financial crisis have meant that they are now outnumbered by a flood of "passive" debtors, who cannot be accused of excessive consumption and carelessly managed credit because their extreme poverty simply means they have no choice: they *must* borrow, to fill their shopping carts with noodles and potatoes. They've lost their jobs and are barely surviving on benefits, or they're single mothers with no qualifications and no prospects beyond perhaps—in the best of cases—finding part-time work that is precarious, poorly paid, and, perversely, financially less advantageous than scraping along as before on whatever help can be found. These people have only debts and no money to pay them. The desk of any *juge d'instance* is stacked high with their files.

And what does he do, the *juge d'instance*? In theory, he doesn't have too much leeway. He can certainly see that on one side there's a poor guy in a stranglehold, on the other a big business with no feelings, but it's not the job of big business to have feelings and it isn't the judge's, either. Between the poor guy and the big business, there's a contract, and the judge's job is to enforce this contract, either by making the debtor pay or by attaching his assets. The problem is that the debtor is usually insolvent and not even attachable, since he possesses what is absolutely necessary for survival. Until the middle of the nineteenth century, this impasse sent the delinquent to debtors' prison, an institution abandoned not for humanitarian reasons but because the upkeep of the prisoners fell to their creditors, not the state, and economic interest eventually outweighed the satisfaction of seeing the guilty punished. Today there is another solution, the overindebtedness commission.

Étienne was still at the ENM in 1989 when the Neiertz Law created these administrative commissions throughout the country to resolve the problem of runaway consumer debt. For Étienne's professor, who equated consumer protection law with undeserved assistance for imbeciles, this was mind-boggling, unheard-of, and judicially scandalous: a law granting the right not to pay one's debts. That was not the object, in theory; the idea was to determine what the overindebted could pay if they tightened their belts as far as they could and to offer them, and their creditors, a debt management plan. In reality, after all the juggling with grace periods, reports, and restructuring, the result was inevitably debt write-off, and this recognition was reaffirmed by another law, passed fifteen years later, when the situation was even worse. Named after its sponsor, the minister for employment, social cohesion, and housing, the Borloo Law of January 2005 instituted a "rehabilitation plan" that extended most of the terms and protections of commercial bankruptcy to individuals, meaning that if upon review of their dossier their situation is deemed "irremediably compromised" (a diagnosis that is fiendishly difficult to determine), their debts are simply written off, and tough luck for their creditors.

Although this development was still in the future when Étienne arrived in Vienne in 1997, consumer associations and some legislators on both the left and the right were actively fighting along those same lines against the lobbying of consumer credit companies, citing the example of Alsace and Moselle, where such provisions had long been the law without the world coming to an end. Their cause was strengthened in 1998 when the Aubry Law legalized partial debt write-off in certain cases, a procedure increasingly favored by the overindebtedness commissions. Were these decisions implemented by the judges? That depended on the judge and on his philosophy of law and life.

I attended a few hearings on overindebtedness in Vienne, presided over by a judge named Jean-Pierre Rieux, Juliette's predecessor, who also filled in for her in the interim after her death. Étienne had worked with him for two years and spoke of him with affection: You'll see, he's the opposite of me, but he knows where he is. "He knows where he is" is the highest compliment Étienne can pay. At first I didn't really get what he meant, but now I understand better, probably because I better understand where I am. Fiftyish, sturdy, a former rugby player, a teacher who became a magistrate late in the game and entered the profession by the back door, Jean-Pierre likes to remind people that until 1958 a *juge d'instance* was called a justice of the peace. That's how he sees his job: conciliation, helping people come to an arrangement among themselves. One of the things Jean-Pierre loved, which is fast disappearing because no one has time for it anymore, is the court's visit to the premises. A plaintiff tells you that the electric gate installed by the Whatsit Company doesn't work. What do you do? You go look at the gate. You get your car, take along your clerk, call up the Whatsit Company so they'll be there too, and with any luck you work out an agreement, get it signed on the spot, then everyone goes off for a drink. This direct approach was not Étienne's style. He was not fond of visiting the premises. What he loved, or rather, what he came to love, was pure law, the subtlety of judicial reasoning, whereas Jean-Pierre describes himself as more of a pragmatist. The law, he says with a shrug, I don't know; I just don't want people to get too badly screwed.

Hearings on overindebtedness, unlike other civil hearings, take place not in the main courtroom but in a small room dubbed the library because a few law books sit around on a shelf there. Formal decorum is not observed; the clerk wears a robe and the traditional white neck cloth, but the judge is in shirtsleeves. You might think you were in the office of the National Employment Bureau or some other social service agency, and what you'd see and hear there would seem to fit that bill.

The situation has only a few variations. A dossier has been submitted to the overindebtedness commission, which may have declared it inadmissible, and that decision is being contested. Or the dossier may have been declared admissible, the commission may have put together a repayment schedule, but one or more creditors may be contesting the schedule because it diminishes or even annuls their claim. Or the commission has found the dossier admissible, there is no disagreement about the repayment plan, and the *juge d'instance* has only to give it final approval.

Before the clerk brings in the debtor, Jean-Paul glances at the cover of the file, which lists the creditors. The length of the list allows him to gauge the extent of the problem. In Mme A.'s case, he nods: he's seen worse.

Forty-five, obese, stuffed into a green and mauve tracksuit, her short hair plastered to her forehead, wearing large fantasy eyeglasses with fluorescent accents, Mme A. is obviously in a tight spot. Questioning her, Jean-Pierre does his best to be reassuring. Cordial, friendly, he says, We'll see what we can do, and his attitude alone indicates that something will indeed be done. Mme A.

earns 950 euros a month as a hospital aide; she has two children
of four and six in her care; she receives child benefits and a rent
subsidy, but since she's started working the subsidy has been
reduced and now covers only a third of her rent. Her situation
became critical three years earlier when she got divorced, because
her expenses then doubled. When Jean-Pierre asks if she has a
car, she senses danger because a car's an asset that can be seized,
and she hurriedly explains that she absolutely needs her car to get
to work. Jean-Pierre replies that her car will not be touched, it's
over ten years old anyway and pardon him for saying so, but it's
worthless. And child care—do you pay someone to watch your
children? Yes, admits Mme A., as if she were ashamed.

On the basis of the information gleaned, the commission has
calculated the percentage of her earnings that can be applied to
the repayment of her debts: 57 euros a month. The debts in question, what with taxes, the Public Housing Company of Vienne
(her landlord), the Crédit Municipal de Lyon, and the credit companies of France-Finances and Cofinoga, amount to 8,675 euros.
The commission has done the math: she can, in ten years, repay
6,840 euros at the most. The commission offers to write off the
remaining 1,835 euros. The problem is to determine who will suffer the loss. The income tax authorities have priority, that's the
law. Next comes the public housing office in Vienne, a social
welfare creditor there's no point in ruining. And so Crédit Municipal, France-Finances, and Cofinoga will take the fall.

The commission has informed all three of its decision; two
have not replied, which means they agree. France-Finances, however, is contesting the decision, and Mme A. is very worried
because they've sent her a nasty letter telling her that they know
she can pay even though she says she can't. You have the letter?
asks Jean-Pierre. Sniffling, Mme A. rummages through the plastic folder she has clung to desperately since she arrived. She hands

the letter to Jean-Pierre, who glances at it, then asks her if anyone has been to see her neighbors or phoned her at work. Yes. Right, says Jean-Pierre. Now, here's what's going to happen. I'm going to hand down my decision in two months, that's the rule, but you I'm going to tell today. I will follow the commission's recommendation. That means I'll write off your debt to France-Finances and they will no longer have the right to send you letters or call you at work or talk to your neighbors. If they do, they'll be the ones breaking the law and you can come see me about it. Your end of it is that you have to pay 57 euros a month to the income tax and public housing people and you *must* pay it, religiously, every month. As long as you do that, as long as you scrupulously follow the schedule, you won't have any problems. The other thing is, you must not take out any new loans. None. You understand? Mme A. understands and goes away relieved.

That one, observes Jean-Pierre after she's closed the door, she'll definitely do everything she can. I'm not saying she'll make it, because with 950 euros a month, two kids on her hands, and the price of gas when you need your car to get to work, plus her expenses going up and housing subsidies going down—well, I wonder how she or any of them manage to survive. They make me laugh, those people who say a repayment schedule is too easy—your debts are now gone, you're home free—when life is actually hell because all you do for ten years is pay and pay, it's impossible to save or borrow anything or buy even the tiniest luxury, and things are calculated so tightly that there's no room for error: the slightest unforeseen expense is catastrophic. The car breaks down, you're dead. Most of the people who come here, let's face it, they'll be back. Her, I hope not, but now take this couple: just look at this list.

* * *

There are a good twenty creditors on the cover of M. and Mme L.'s dossier: the usual banks, moneylenders, credit companies, but also garage owners, small businessmen—they've run up tabs everywhere and although the individual amounts are all small, the total is impressive. The couple comes in; they're both in their thirties. He's emaciated, ashen, his face constantly twitching, while she's chubby, with blotchy skin. Mme A. had seemed on the verge of tears throughout her hearing, but this woman seems well beyond that, sunk in apathy. They've recently separated but are facing their creditors together. She's kept the apartment, where she lives with their four children; he sleeps in their broken-down car. Lately she'd been working as a waitress and he as a door-to-door salesman, trying to sell fire extinguishers weighing well over a hundred pounds to elderly people who couldn't even lift them. He's been let go because he wasn't making enough sales and she couldn't go on because their car quit running, her shift ended late at night, and there was no bus to get home. They're both HIV positive. With massive debt, their resources reduced to social services, and their hopes for a "return to better times" (to use the current legal catchphrase) at just about zero, the question is why they weren't prodded into personal bankruptcy, which would write off all their debts in accordance with the Borloo Law, rather than sent to the overindebtedness commission, which can't go as far as that. They owe close to 20,000 euros. Their ability to repay has been evaluated, God knows how, at 31 euros a month. That's enough to set up a schedule over 120 months that hasn't the slightest chance of being followed. But that's fine with this couple, who are clearly exhausted; all they want is a truce, a few weeks safe from the collection agencies that despite their obvious insolvency have brought out the big guns: the bright red final-notice envelopes in their mailbox, the neighbors obligingly informed of their difficulties, and even the visit to the children on Wednesday afternoon, when school lets out early, to tell them to pass on the message to Mama and Papa: If they don't pay what they owe, you'll be thrown out of your home. Mama and Papa love you, they don't want you to sleep in the street, so ask them to pay what they owe and maybe they'll listen to you, their own children.

Perhaps you think I'm overdoing it, says Jean-Pierre, but that's really what happens, and the worst part is that the poor bastards who do this crappy work are in trouble themselves. He sees them come up before the commission week after week, and if he asks what they do for a living, that's it: they work part-time for collection agencies—and when his jaw drops they don't even understand why. So Jean-Pierre asks M. and Mme L. if personal bankruptcy wouldn't be better for them, seeing as it would dispose of all their debts, but they say no, they've already put together a dossier, they're too tired to start over. Jean-Pierre sighs and says, Fine. But have you really looked at your repayment schedule? You do understand that you have to repay 31 euros every month? Yes, they reply, and I have the feeling he could have said 310 or 310,000 euros, they'd have still said yes. Before letting them leave, Jean-Pierre tries to ascertain whether the social services are really following up on them, whether there are people the couple can talk to, and they say yes, yes, then leave as if they can't stand to be in that room a moment longer, having to answer these questions and participate in one of life's crueler rituals of humiliation. Their plan for getting out of debt had been sent to all their creditors, along with a formal notice of that day's hearing. Only one of the credit companies has contested the plan, but without sending a representative to the hearing, having probably and with reason considered their cause lost in advance. When the clerk goes to get the next people, however, she returns in some surprise with a gentleman in a checked shirt who has also turned up for the L. hearing. He'd received the notice, so he came. He works for Intermarché, the

chain supermarket, which is suing over two bad checks for 280
euros. When I hear that, I think, Intermarché can certainly afford
to lose 280 euros, but as usual things aren't that simple, because
in this case "Intermarché" means a superette franchisee in Saint-
Jean-de-Bournay, a village not far from Rosier, and the man in
the checked shirt is not at all a heartless representative of the
huge chain but a poor guy who personally has to take the hit when
checks bounce and who's now out 280 euros. He's just encountered the delinquent couple as they left, has recognized them, and,
with a rueful look, admits, It's true they don't seem too well off.
You said it, confirms Jean-Pierre with a sigh, so I'm not going to
lie to you. Here's the situation: they have a long list of creditors,
almost no income, four children, so . . . So? repeats the franchisee. So you were sent their repayment schedule yourself. The
Banque de France has proposed paying certain claims and writing off the others. After a silence, the franchisee says, Ah . . .
that's one solution, I guess. A solution he obviously finds unpal-
atable, and he seems particularly shocked to hear it defended by
a judge. Jean-Pierre then rises and, carrying the schedule, goes
around the table to sit next to the franchisee and explain something: Mind you, it's not hopeless. The schedule covers 120
months, which seems a bit ambitious to me, frankly, given the
precariousness of their lives. But you see, what's on offer for you
is not a simple write-off. The offer is, nothing at all for 53 months,
while they pay off the main creditors, and then 31 euros for the
next nine months. It's not impossible that you could recuper-
ate your money in a little over five years. I can't promise you
this, I don't know where they'll be in five years, but it's possible.
The franchisee leaves not exactly reassured but not disgusted,
either.

* * *

Étienne learned to be a *juge d'instance* at Jean-Pierre's side. Deep down, they were in agreement. They thought credit companies went too far and they didn't mind when they got a chance to give them a hard time. But as judges they were basically tinkering, dealing with matters on a case-by-case basis, without trying to establish jurisprudence.* Then Étienne learned that another *juge d'instance*, Philippe Florès, had made his courtroom in Niort a model of consumer protection. Étienne knows his own worth, does not pretend to be modest, and that's why—he says—he is never afraid to ask when he doesn't know or to copy others who know better than he does. He therefore contacted Florès and began to apply his methods, which were more systematic than those of Jean-Pierre.

Florès had finished the ENM at the same time as Étienne but had become a *juge d'instance* right away, just when the over-indebtedness commissions were being set up. And in spite of or because of the fact that he came from a poor family, the commissions had shocked Florès, too. They went against everything he'd been taught for years about respecting contracts and understanding that the law isn't made for idiots who don't read what they sign. On that last point, he quickly changed his mind: the law is also made for idiots, and for the ignorant, and for

---

* The United States uses the common law system that evolved among anglophone peoples, a system firmly established by custom before laws were written down and codified, and the injustices of which could eventually be amended through the petitions of citizens. In a way, common law grows from the bottom up. France, by contrast, uses the civil legal system, in which legislation is the primary source of laws, which thus spring not from a catalog of judicial decisions but from written codes and statutes that must then be strictly applied to the legal problems of daily life. In such a system, law develops from the top down.

So while the American common law system explicitly acknowledges case law as a major source of jurisprudence—judges in selected courts may interpret and make law through decisions that can be cited as precedents—law in France is statutory, and French judges may not make law, only narrowly interpret it. The radical effort of "the judges in Vienne" to render justice by actually creating jurisprudence should be understood within this context.

everyone who has, yes, signed a contract but who has also been royally screwed.

There was one law on the books, though, that did try to limit predatory contracts: the Scrivener Law of 1978, a basically social-democratic measure that limited—in connection with certain credit transactions—the sacrosanct powers of contracts.

In pure orthodox economic reasoning, people are free, equal, and grown-up enough to enter into agreements with one another without having the state get involved, and a landlord has a perfect right to offer his tenant a lease that allows him to evict the tenant or double his rent whenever he wants, to require that he turn off the lights at seven every evening or wear a nightshirt instead of pajamas—and as long as the tenant has the corresponding right to reject the lease, all is well. The law, however, takes reality into account: the parties are not actually as free and equal as free market ideology claims. One owns, the other asks; one has a choice, the other less so—which is why landlord-tenant leases are regulated, and loans as well. On the one hand, credit must be encouraged because it fuels the economy; on the other, people must be protected from exploitation because that degrades the social contract. The Scrivener Law therefore declares abusive all clauses that render a contract unconscionable and imposes upon the lender, since he's the one drawing it up, a number of formal requirements, set phrases, obligatory clauses, standards of legibility and clarity—in short, a few rules aimed at ensuring that the borrower at least understands what he's getting into.

The problem with the Scrivener Law was that the consumer credit companies it was intended to regulate didn't respect it and the consumers it was supposed to protect knew nothing about it. Florès knew it backward and forward and unilaterally decided, off in his corner, to make sure it was respected. Nothing more, but nothing less.

Most of his colleagues, opening the dossier of a big credit company like Cofinoga vs. Mme Whosis, simply determined that yes, Mme Whosis was no longer paying the monthly sums mandated by her contract; and yes, Cofinoga was entitled by contract to demand repayment of the principal plus interest and penalties; and yes, Mme Whosis was broke but the law is the law, contracts are contracts, and even though I might find it distressing I have no choice, as a judge, but to render an enforceable decision: to seize the delinquent party's assets or direct her to the overindebtedness commission.

As for Florès, he would hardly glance at what Mme Whosis owed but would zero in on the contract, in which he often found abusive clauses and almost always spotted technical irregularities. For example, the law requires a contract to be set in eight-point type; this one wasn't. By law its renewal must be offered by letter; that hadn't happened. Florès had drawn up a little chart of the most common irregularities; he would check them off and, at the hearing, declare: This contract is worthless. Cofinoga's lawyer would gape at him, and if he had the nerve he'd reply, Monsieur le Président, it's none of your business. It's the responsibility of the defaulting party—or her lawyer, if she has one—to raise such objections, but you cannot do so in her stead. File an appeal, Florès would reply.

In the meantime, he would grant Cofinoga the right to reclaim its capital, but not the interest and penalties. Well, normally the borrower's payments are first applied to the interest, not the capital. But if the judge decides that he must repay *only* the capital and that what he has *already* repaid is capital, the judge might find himself telling the borrower, You no longer owe (let's say) 1,500 euros, you owe 600. And sometimes it would be nothing at all, and sometimes Cofinoga even owed the borrower money. Mme Whosis would faint with joy.

* * *

Philippe Florès, in Niort, pioneered that legal tactic. Étienne, in
Vienne, was soon following suit. (I'd written "matching him," but
Étienne wrote in the margin of the manuscript, "That's stretching
it!" Duly noted.) He applied such remedies to his heart's content
in civil proceedings and especially in those concerning overindebtedness, where his passion for ferreting out irregularities and
declaring the forfeiture of interest radically changed the deal.
From the unfortunate debtor's point of view, there's a great difference between being told that one's financial situation is so
untenable that the only option is to write off what one owes, and
hearing, You have been wronged and I will remedy this wrong.
That's much pleasanter, both to hear and to say, and Étienne did
not deprive himself of that pleasure. Besides, once the total debt
was reduced, it became possible to put together repayment sched-
ules that were infinitely more realistic. There again, it was up to
the judge to decide who would be reimbursed first, who might be
repaid later, if possible, and who would get nothing. The decision
was essentially political. The reason some got nothing was not
simply because there were no funds available but also because
they did not deserve reimbursement. Because they had behaved
badly, because they were the bad guys, because it's only right that
the swindler should sometimes get swindled. Of course, Étienne
doesn't state matters that crudely. Regarding the creditors, he
prefers to distinguish between those who will be seriously hurt
by the denial of their claim and those who will suffer less: between
the small garage owner, the private moneylender, the modest franchisee in Saint-Jean-de-Bournay, who, if they are not paid, could
themselves fall into financial ruin, and the big lending institutions
and insurance companies, which factor the risk of nonpayment
into all their contracts anyway. The rationale that Étienne prefers
is that the small tradesman, the garage owner, the franchisee, once
burned, might become mistrustful, no longer willing to give any-

one a break, and that the social fabric would be that little bit more frayed. He says that before anything else, his job as a judge is to help safeguard the bonds of society, so that people can continue to live together.

Still, even Jean-Pierre was beginning to think Étienne was overdoing it. Half jokingly, he called him Robespierre and the little pinko judge. It's too easy, he said, and above all it isn't a judge's job to divide the world into cynical big corporations and poor naïve victims—and then go all out to serve only those victims. Étienne countered by echoing Florès: I'm only applying the law. And in fact he was applying it, but in his own way and in the spirit of a text that had impressed him, Oswald Baudot's controversial "Harangue to New Magistrates," which offers judges this counsel (and here I paraphrase): Be partial. To maintain the balance between the strong and the weak, the rich and the poor, who do not weigh the same, tip the balance a little to one side. Incline more favorably toward the wife than the husband, the debtor than the creditor, the worker than the boss, the injured than the injurer's insurance company, the thief than the police, the litigant than justice. The law may be interpreted; it will say what you want it to say. Between the robber and the robbed, do not be afraid to punish the robbed.

As for the lawyers for the banks and credit companies, they left hearings both crestfallen and furious, forced to explain to their clients that the reason they'd lost, when they used to win all such cases, was because there was a son of a bitch in the courtroom in Vienne, some one-legged judge who measured font sizes and said, Sorry, it isn't eight-point type, so bye-bye interest and penalties. If the eight-point ploy didn't work, he'd come up with something else. No contract found favor in his eyes. Elsewhere in the *département*, in Bourgoin, there was a *tribunal d'instance* where the judge operated totally differently: creditors always left his hearings with a smile. The lawyers began scrambling to get around the territorial assignments and bring their cases before that understanding man. Hard on the poor, soft on the rich, Étienne used to joke, but that's certainly not how the judge in Bourgoin saw himself; he would have said the same thing as Étienne and Florès: I apply the law. And his way of applying it, in 1998 or 1999, was still largely the norm. The judges in Niort and Vienne were considered, even by their colleagues, as leftists and weirdos. And yet, things were beginning to change.

According to Florès, only about 2 percent of credit card customers default on their loans. It's a marginal amount, already accounted for, no big deal. What is a big deal is the risk of contamination. The credit companies are well aware that 90 percent of their contracts violate the law, technically speaking. As long as France has just two or three judges who pick up on this and use it to deny them interest income, that's all right, and such decisions are often reversed on appeal in any case. If there are fifty or a hundred judges like that, it's a different story. One that's going to get very expensive.

Such a prospect filled Philippe Florès and Étienne with joy. They saw themselves as little Davids confronting the Goliath of credit and as trailblazers who would inevitably win over their colleagues. They passed copies of their decisions around within the Association des Juges d'Instance, trying to convert the unenlightened. Each new recruit was a victory, bringing them closer to the critical point at which jurisprudence would be transformed and banks would tremble on their foundations.

* * *

Étienne felt a thrill of triumph one day when representatives of a large credit company asked to meet him, and he gave them an appointment. Four men arrived at his office: two company managers, one of whom had come all the way from Paris, and two lawyers from Vienne. I would like to describe their meeting as if it were a scene in a detective novel. It would begin quietly, with an exchange of banter: So you're the guy who's gumming up the works? But the jokes turn vaguely menacing, then give way to blunt threats and attempted bribery. One of the visitors, in a suit and fedora, talks while striding up and down. The one-legged judge keeps cool, biding his time. The gunsels hover silently in the background. Finally, the man who's talking stops in front of the judge and mutters through clenched teeth, I'm going to crush you. He picks up some small ornament, breaks it with his pale, nervous hands, and drops the pieces onto the desk, warning, I'm going to crush you *like this*.

Actually, that's not at all what happened. The conversation was polite and professional. The visitors acknowledged their discomfort with the decisions coming from Vienne and their fears of just what Florès was hoping for, that the whole thing would snowball. Besides which, they saw these verdicts as dangerous: if matters continued in that vein, credit would become impossible, and then where would everyone be? They'd come not to expound on judicial disagreements, however, but to seek advice. What could they do to avoid any future reversals? How could they do things according to the rules?

Simple, answered Étienne, slightly surprised. The law is there. Respect it.

His visitors sighed. It's complicated . . .

What's complicated? The law says that the contract must be

drawn up in eight-point type and it almost never is, so I'm taking advantage of that to shoot down your interest charges. You can say I'm nitpicking. But instead tell me why, since you know the rule and it's easy to apply, you still don't apply it. I have my own idea about the answer: it suits you that the contracts are hard to read. Here's something else. Why don't you ever send out letters offering to renew your contracts? Is it because you consider them renewed by tacit agreement, which—let me just point out—is also against the law? I can tell you why, because one of your own people told me. (In fact, this was Florès, whose friends in the loan industry kept him abreast of insider gossip.) Because when you did send out those letters, you had a 30 percent cancellation rate. And that's really annoying. Experience tells us that a dormant credit card will get used sooner or later, whereas a canceled card is a dead loss. And why do you never mention the interest rates except in tiny letters squirreled away on the back of a flashy brochure? You know why. Because they're horrendous, your interest rates—18 percent, 19 percent, more than the usury rate—and you slip that mickey to people who would never sign up if they realized what you were doing.

That's where you're wrong, replied the man from Paris. They sign anyway because they have no choice. Sure you can say they'd be better off taking out a standard loan, but those standard loans—the problem is our clients can't get them. It's like insuring your car when you've got so many points on your license that no one will take you: of course it's expensive. You keep talking about information. You tell us we don't give our clients enough information about what they're getting into, then you accuse us of not gathering enough information about our clients' ability to repay us. But our clients, what they want is money, not information that dissuades them from borrowing it. And what we want is to earn money by loaning it, not to collect information that persuades us not to lend it. We're only doing our job. Credit exists, and you, what you're doing with your constant quibbling about the way our contracts look, is really complaining about *advertising*, which is always like that. In big letters it says: Buy your car for 30 euros a month, but there's an asterisk, and down below—in small print you've got to look at carefully, true—there are clauses saying that it costs a little more than 30 euros a month or else that the offer's valid at certain times but not others. Everyone knows this, people aren't fools. But you, if I've got this straight, you want a world without advertising, without credit, maybe without TV, too, because we all know TV rots people's brains . . .

Of course, Étienne said with a smile, and by the way, I spend my vacations in North Korea. No, I'm fine with a world where people have the right to break the law. But I also want, as a judge, the right to make people respect it. Isn't that what liberalism is?

16

One thing makes Étienne laugh when he talks about meeting Juliette: what went through his mind the first time he saw her. Someone knocked on his door; he said, Come in, and when he looked up, she was coming toward him on crutches. Wow! he thought. A gimp!

It's not having *had* the thought that makes him laugh but that it just popped up ready-made in those three exact words, he swears— including the "Wow!" A moment later, above the crutches he saw a pleasing face, a lovely smile, something open, joyous, and grave, but what came first were the crutches. Her way of coming toward him on those crutches—he took that right away as a gift. And he immediately felt happy to be able to give her a present in return, and so simply: he merely stood up and came out from behind his desk to show her that even though he didn't have crutches, he limped, too.

17

When I decided to go to Vienne in early autumn to hang around the courthouse and see what a *juge d'instance* does, I realized that it was time to phone Patrice. Since only Hélène and Étienne knew anything about my project, I was apprehensive about that call. In the event, he seemed a little surprised to hear from me, but not at all suspicious. Just come to the house, he said.

He was waiting for me on the station platform, holding Diane in his arms, and asked if I'd mind coming along while he did some shopping. The girls usually came home for lunch, so he had to fix them three meals a day, three meals for three little girls, the youngest only one and a half, but he never lost his patience, raising his voice only slightly whenever they were being too naughty. Back at the house, I jumped right in to help, fetching the groceries from the trunk, setting and clearing the table, loading and emptying the dishwasher, wiping off the yellow Formica table, cleaning up the rice and yogurt launched by Diane from her high chair, and in an hour I felt like part of the household. Patrice welcomed my presence calmly, and neither he nor the girls seemed to wonder why I was there. After lunch, he put Diane down for her nap, Amélie and Clara walked across the square to school, and we men went to sit under the catalpa in the garden with our coffees. We talked of this and that, about how their life was organized now that Juliette was gone. Patrice seemed neither curious nor anxious about why I was visiting him. I'd come to spend a few days with them, we were chatting over coffee—it was as simple as that. On the train to Vienne I'd wondered what tack I might take to get things started, but now I wasn't worried at all. Finishing my coffee, I pulled out my notebook, as I had in Étienne's kitchen, and said, Now I'd like you to talk to me about Juliette. And to begin with, about yourself.

His father, a tall, dry, austere fellow with a full set of chin whiskers, is a math teacher, and his mother an elementary school teacher who left her job to raise their children. The couple's love of mountains took them first to the town of Albertville, in the Savoie, and later to a village near Bourg-Saint-Maurice, where they bought a house. A militant ecologist right from the start, his father is the sworn enemy of huge ski resorts, advertising, television (which he refuses to have), and consumer society in general. His three sons, who admired him, also feared him a little. Their mother spoiled them, wanted them to be confident and outgoing little boys, and Patrice feels—without any resentment—that she protected them a bit too much, at least in his case. For example,

since he was afraid of being bullied, she decided he wasn't ready
for secondary school and had him repeat his last year of primary
education. When he and his brothers were children, everything
was fine, and they had a group of boys with whom they played
cowboys and Indians in the village streets. But things changed
with adolescence. Halfway through secondary school, their friends
began dropping out, which was not an option for Patrice and his
brothers. The other boys had mopeds, they smoked and chased
girls; the brothers did not, and true to their parents' values, they
thought their pals were wasting their lives. Instead of going dancing on Saturday nights, they listened to records in their bedroom
with the lights out: Pink Floyd and Graeme Allwright, a singer-
songwriter who moved to France from New Zealand in his early
twenties and translated songs by Leonard Cohen into French.
The brothers didn't feel superior, but they did feel different. Their
friends, whom they still see today, are garage mechanics, masons,
ski-rental guys, or ski-slope groomers at Bourg-Saint-Maurice.
Patrice's two brothers became elementary school teachers like their
mother and still live in Savoie, while Patrice is a cartoonist in the
neighboring *département* of Isère. None of them has wandered far
from home or succeeded—or failed—spectacularly, yet the differences remain. After Diane's nap, when we took her to the
nanny who watches her for a few hours in the afternoon, Patrice
mentioned that the woman and her husband don't live the way his
own little family does, meaning that they always have the TV on,
are avid soccer fans, and lean to the right politically, maybe even
the extreme right. Having said that, he added that they were wonderful people and I was sure he meant it, sure that his observations on their values reflected no disdain, none of the snobbism
that can be all the more intense when the actual differences are
rather small. Patrice just goes on talking to his neighbors about the
global justice movement or currency transaction taxes, without

much success but without any doubt that he's right and without any contempt for those who don't share his views and who feel there are too many foreigners in France.

Patrice wasn't very good in school and admits he was lazy. He liked to daydream off in his corner about imaginary lives in worlds peopled with knights, giants, and princesses. He gave form to these reveries by writing his own versions of those books in which "YOU Are the Hero." When he flunked his baccalaureate exam, he refused to repeat his last year of school, because nothing he'd learned there interested him. The problem was that nothing else interested him either, no profession except, after he'd thought about it, drawing comic strips. Finally, he'd found an answer to the embarrassing question, What do you want to do when you grow up? It was a refuge rather than a true vocation, he admits, a way of keeping at bay a real world in which you must be strong and struggle to succeed. His parents agreed to send him to Paris, where he shared an attic room with a cousin and worked on the drawings that he hoped would be his entrée into publishing. With hindsight, he regrets not going to art school and thereby passing up the chance to acquire a solid technical foundation. He was a complete autodidact, drawing in ballpoint on sheets of graph paper, ignorant of almost everything that was happening in his chosen field. He was familiar with Tintin, the medieval adventurers Johan and Peewit, the little bellboy Spirou, the cowboy and Civil War veteran Blueberry—and he left it at that. Sometimes he'd leaf through comics for adults in a bookstore, but just looking at those aggressive, sophisticated images seemed to betray the childlike world he still cherished. Patrice used to wander around Paris with his cousin, another romantic, who was studying the viola. Occasionally they'd go to the Parc de Sceaux, just south of Paris, climb a tree, and stay there all day, dreaming about the princess they were each going to find. After a year, though, Patrice was ready to write "The End" on the last panel of his comic book and have a try at selling it. The fellow he saw at Casterman, the publisher of Franco-Belgian comics, told him gently that his work was not bad but too naïve, too sentimental. Patrice left with his portfolio under his arm, disappointed yet not really surprised. He didn't knock on any other doors. The world of comics was tougher than the world of *his* comics.

When he was old enough for military service, he never considered either signing up for alternative service like any middle-class youth with common sense or getting himself rejected on medical grounds the way the bourgeois rebels did. He was staunchly anti-war, so naturally he became a conscientious objector, serving the army in a noncombat role. He wound up doing vaguely medieval-looking animation in a château near Clermont-Ferrand, which he might have enjoyed if his colleagues hadn't turned out to be as vulgar and foulmouthed as any soldiers, and after that Patrice worked on career-choice brochures in a state publishing house, devoting his talent to illustrating little dialogues for teaching language skills. Released from the army after two years, he registered at the National Employment Agency, which found him a job as a delivery driver. He moved into a studio apartment in Cachan, in the southern suburbs of Paris. Objectively speaking, he had good reason to worry about his future, but he didn't. Career plans were not his thing, and neither was worrying.

At a community arts center in the 5th arrondissement, Patrice signed up for an amateur theater class that focused on improvisation and body expression exercises, which suited him much more than acting in real plays. The students would put on some New Agey music and lie on foam rubber mats on the floor, their only instruction to let themselves go. They'd start out curled up, then begin to move, slowly unfolding like a flower turning toward the sun, reaching out to the other students, coming into contact with them. It was magic. Other exercises, for two people, would be to stand looking into each other's eyes while trying to express an emotion: suspicion, trust, fear, desire . . . Patrice learned from this theatrical experience how ill at ease he was in his relations with other people. He was a handsome young man, as I could see in the photos he showed me, but he describes himself as having been a pimply scarecrow with a brand-new beard, granny glasses, an Afro, and scarves knitted by his mother. The theater brought him out of himself. It was a path to other people and, above all, to girls. He'd grown up in a brotherhood of boys, and not only had he never slept with a girl, but he literally did not know any. Thanks to that theater course, he met some. He invited a few to cafés and the movies, but his romanticism included a Puritan streak and girls who seemed too liberated scared him off. That's when Juliette showed up.

Whenever Hélène told me that she'd been jealous of Juliette, who was the prettiest of the three sisters, I'd shake my head. I'd seen Juliette sick, I'd seen her dying, I'd seen childhood photos in which she and Hélène looked almost like twins. But in the ones Patrice showed me, Juliette was in fact extraordinarily lovely, with a large, sensual mouth and a toothy smile, like Julia Roberts, and that smile was not only radiant, which everyone says about her, but voracious, almost carnivorous. Sociable, funny, at ease with people, she had a charisma that ought to have discouraged a boy like Patrice. Luckily, there were those crutches. They made her accessible.

They didn't go out alone at first, only as part of the group. The teacher took them to the theater, where there were stairs Juliette couldn't climb. Patrice, shy but well built, carried Juliette upstairs in his arms, and from then on that was the rule. One carrying the other, they went up all the stairs they encountered. Soon the two of them began visiting monuments, preferably those with many floors, and when they sat next to each other in darkened theaters, they started holding hands. They were both very sensitive about hands, Patrice remembers. Their fingers would exchange caresses and twine together for hours, and it was never the same, always new, always deeply moving. He hardly dared believe this miracle was happening to him. Then they kissed. Then they made love. He undressed her, she was naked in his arms; gently he moved her almost motionless legs. For both of them, it was the first time.

Patrice had found the princess of his dreams. Smart, beautiful, too smart and beautiful for him, he thought, and yet with her everything was simple. He needn't fear any calculated flirting, or deception, or treachery. He could be himself with her, without being afraid she might take advantage of his naïveté. They both took what was happening to them seriously. They were in love. And so they would be husband and wife.

Still, in the beginning the differences in their characters worried them, especially Juliette. Not only did Patrice have no real profession but he wasn't concerned about it. Earning enough to live on by driving delivery vans or running a comics workshop in a Ville de Paris recreation center was fine with him. Juliette, however, was energetic and determined. She attached great importance to her studies, so it bothered her that Patrice was such a dreamer, so easygoing. And it bothered Patrice that she was studying law and, what's more, at the Université Panthéon-Assas, the most elite law school in the country and a hotbed of fascists. Though he wasn't politically active, Patrice called himself an anarchist and considered

the law nothing but an instrument of repression in the service of
the rich and powerful. Now, if Juliette had wanted to be a lawyer,
to defend widows and orphans, he could have understood, but a
judge! At one point, Juliette had actually thought about joining
the bar and had earned a master's in business law, but her courses
had disgusted her. The professors taught their students sneaky
ways to help future clients make huge profits and how to extract
fat retainers in return. This open alliance with the law of the
jungle, the smiling cynicism of her teachers and fellow students
all proved the correctness of Patrice's contemptuous diatribes.
Patiently, Juliette explained that she loved the law because in the
contest between the weak and the strong it's the law that protects and freedom that enslaves, and if she wanted to become a
judge it was to make others respect the law, not pervert it. Patrice
understood in theory, but still, being married to a judge would be
hard for him to swallow.

The difference between their backgrounds was another sticking point. Juliette lived with her parents, and every time he went
to see her at their spacious apartment in Montparnasse he felt
desperately uncomfortable. Both distinguished scientists, Jacques
and Marie-Aude were Catholics, elitists, right-leaning, and in their
home Patrice felt looked down on—the provincial boy whose
schoolteacher parents drove around in battered heaps plastered
with anti–nuclear power stickers. His folks had a rule: You can
discuss anything, in fact you must discuss everything, for from
discussion comes enlightenment. As far as Juliette's parents were
concerned (and mine, moreover), a Savoyard ecologist who believed
microwave ovens were dangerous was as impossible to reason with
as someone who claimed the sun revolved around the earth, and
a flat earth at that. As they saw it, opinions were not equally worthy of consideration, there were simply people who knew and
people who didn't, and there was no point in acting as if a meaning-

ful discussion were possible. Granted, Patrice was nice enough, he sincerely loved Juliette, but he represented everything they loathed: long hair, that 1968 antiauthoritarian foolishness, and, worst of all, failure. They saw him as a loser and could not accept the fact that their gifted daughter was in love with one. Patrice's hostility had more general, abstract targets: big capital, religion as the opium of the people, an overweening faith in science, but it wasn't in his character to apply aversions in principle to actual people. The contempt he sensed on the part of his future in-laws disarmed him: he could not feel contempt for them in return but simply thought he'd have been better off if he'd never met them. But he had, and he loved Juliette, so they'd just have to work things out.

I think Juliette suffered more from this contempt than he did, because she was indeed her parents' daughter and couldn't help seeing Patrice through their eyes. She wasn't the type to pretend to herself. She'd chosen him with her eyes wide open. But before she had, she'd hesitated. She must have imagined, very thoroughly, in a bright and even cruel light, what spending her life with Patrice would be like. On the one hand, the limits this choice would impose on her. And on the other, the bedrock support he would give her. The certainty of being loved absolutely, of always being carried.

Even Patrice began to ask himself questions. The law, her parents, the need to succeed—none of that was for him. With Juliette, he was too far from his roots. And anyway, was it reasonable to settle down with a handicapped wife without ever having known another woman? He told me that one day they talked and came to the reasonable conclusion that they weren't made to live together. They told each other why. Patrice talked the most, it was always like that with them. He said whatever went through his head, whatever he felt in his heart, freely, whereas with Juliette you

never really knew what she was thinking. After talking, they
resolved to separate, and began to cry. They cried for two hours in
each other's arms on the narrow bed in the little room in Cachan,
and while they were crying they each realized that there wasn't any
sorrow they couldn't survive together, that the only inconsolable
sorrow was precisely the one they were inflicting on themselves
that very moment. So they said no, they would not separate, they
would live together, would never leave each other, and that's exactly
what they did.

Juliette let her parents know she accepted their disapproval of
her choice but required them to respect it, and the couple moved
into a tiny studio apartment on the ninth floor of a crummy
building in the 13th arrondissement. When the elevator was out
of order, which was often, Patrice carried Juliette up the stairs. A
few floors below them was a center for ex-cons, for whom Juliette
did pro bono work. She made it a point of honor not to ask for
money from her family, and the two of them lived on very little:
Juliette's disability pension and the freelance work Patrice did on
comic strips in a magazine for phone card collectors. Later they
lived in Bordeaux, where Juliette studied at the ENM almost ten
years after Étienne. She was brilliant and, as always, much loved.
One of Patrice's drawings, representing Marianne—a national
symbol of France—with Juliette's features, was chosen as the
emblem of her graduating class. Amélie was born. When Juliette
graduated from the university, she chose civil law, the *tribunal
d'instance*, and Vienne, because she'd made sure the courthouse
there had an elevator.

18

The more Patrice told me, that afternoon beneath the catalpa, the more astonished I was by how much he trusted me. It wasn't me in particular; he would have trusted anyone else the same way, because he'd never learned to be on his guard. An unknown quantity, a writer brother-in-law, the author of supposedly dark and cruel books, had turned up at his house to write another one about his dead wife and had asked him for the story of his life, so he'd complied. He didn't try to make himself look good, or bad, either. He played no role, didn't care what I thought. He wasn't proud or ashamed of himself. Consenting to be defenseless gave him great strength. About him as well, Étienne says with admiration: He knows where he is.

* * *

Amélie and Clara came home from school and the four of us went off on bikes to pick up Diane at her nanny's house. Patrice had a seat on his bicycle baggage rack for Clara, but Amélie already knew how to ride on her own without training wheels. We crossed the street, passed the school, then the church, and turned onto the little road leading to the cemetery. It was really the country there, with hills, dales, cows. Shall we go say hi to Mama? suggested Patrice. We leaned the bikes against the cemetery wall; Patrice picked up Clara. Juliette's grave was covered with loose earth and surrounded by big round stones brightly painted by the village children, who had written their names on their stones. I thought back to the funeral.

Patrice had read a simple, moving text in church, saying he had lost his beloved. Étienne had then read some fierce words telling us death was not a gentle thing. Finally Hélène had read the text I'd seen her compose, saying that Juliette's quiet little life had been neither quiet nor little but fully chosen and lived to the full. There'd also been a kind of homily delivered by Juliette's godfather, who was a deacon and had lost his own daughter to cancer. Étienne told me later he hadn't liked the kindly Catholic smiles with which the man had announced that Juliette was now with the Father and we should rejoice in that, but Étienne also understood that some people were comforted by such thoughts, so why not? The funeral procession had followed the route I'd just taken with Patrice and the girls and had lacked solemnity, but that was all right. There had been no hearse; pallbearers had simply carried Juliette's coffin. Many children and young couples were part of the procession, for it was the funeral of a young woman. Things had gotten slightly out of hand at the graveside because Patrice, who had also been irritated by the deacon's speech and what he considered sanctimonious crap, had announced that now we could all say good-bye to Juliette in whatever way we wanted. Back at the church, he'd already removed the cross lying on the coffin. Like his family, Patrice believes in sincerity and spontaneity in all circumstances; that's how he lives and it's good for him, but without the decorum provided by religious ritual, the ceremony fell apart. Instead of everyone filing by to toss a bit of earth on the coffin, people wandered around at a loss, not daring to say a personal farewell, perhaps not even knowing how. Some mourners crowded around the grave, and the children tried to find places for the stones they'd been told to paint in school. To reintroduce a little order, one believer intoned a Hail Mary, but only a few others joined in. Most people left the cemetery to gather on the road in small groups, silent and upset; some were already smoking, no one knew whether the funeral was over or not, and it was the gravedigger who decided the matter by bringing over his backhoe to fill in the grave and make an end of it.

Whenever Patrice bears the responsibility for a social occasion, he handles it poorly, I think, but alone with his daughters and me he was completely natural, his words simple and correct, and I felt such visits to the cemetery must be soothing to the girls. In her father's arms, Clara was quiet, but Amélie made what seemed her customary tour of the neighboring graves, which she found less pretty than her mother's. I don't like marble, she said, I think it's sad, and her slightly affected tone suggested both that she was repeating something she'd heard a grown-up say and that she said it at every visit, because the repetition made her feel better. I looked at her and wondered if I would still be in touch with her when she was an adult. If I were to write this book, then probably yes. Would I still be with Hélène then? Would we have had some joint role in the girls' education, as Hélène so fervently hoped would happen? Would we have taken them off each year for a vacation, and not just that first summer after their mother died? In ten years, Amélie would be a young lady in whose life I would perhaps have a role, a kind of uncle who had written a book about her parents in which she had appeared as a little girl. I imagined her reading this book and felt that while I was writing it, she and her two sisters were looking on.

After dinner, I read a story to Clara to put her to sleep. It concerned a little toad who is all alone in the dark, frightened by strange noises, and goes to seek comfort in the bed of his mama and papa. Me, said Clara, I don't have a mama anymore. My mama's dead. That's true, I said, and could think of nothing to add. I thought of my own children, of the stories I read to them when they were little. Hélène and I had almost had a child, which she'd lost right after her sister's death, and I thought sadly that we probably wouldn't ever have another. I remembered Clara during the week she and Amélie spent with us that summer. She kept saying, When we get home, maybe Mama will be there. She couldn't help imagining that at some point the door would open and her mama would be waiting on the threshold. I thought it was a good thing, those frequent visits to the grave: at least there was a place where her mama *was*, a place that wasn't everywhere and nowhere. In time, she would no longer be behind every door.

After the girls were in bed, Patrice and I went down to his studio in the basement, where he had made up a bed for me. He talked about a comic strip he was planning, one of his usual stories about knights and princesses, to be entitled "The Paladin." Really? The Paladin? I smiled, and he laughed a little ruefully, but proudly, too, as if to say, I am what I am. In the meantime, he had a commission, some sketches for a story set in a kennel with a half dozen dogs, familiar character types like the grumpy Rottweiler, the stuck-up poodle, the muscle-bound Dalmatian who likes to show off, the adorable mutt—who I suspected would be the noble hero of these tales. When I said as much, Patrice gave that same little laugh, meaning, Nice going, you got me: paladin and simpleton, that's me. I looked at the drawings, one by one: a comic strip for children, a bit old-fashioned but drawn with a delicate and confident hand, and with incredible modesty. I should say, with incomprehensible modesty, because it's a trait I can't understand. I'm ambitious, I worry, I have to believe that what I'm writing is exceptional, that it will be admired, and I get excited believing this but collapse when I lose faith. Not Patrice. He enjoys drawing but doesn't believe his work is exceptional and doesn't need to believe it to live at peace with himself. Neither does he try to change his style. That would be as impossible for him as changing his dreams: he has no control there. I decided that in this respect he was an artist.

While we were examining his drawings, the phone rang. Ah! Antoine! exclaimed Patrice. So, are congratulations in order? They were. Laure, Antoine's wife, had just given birth to their first child, a son. Arthur? That's a great name, Arthur. Standing next to Patrice on the phone with Juliette's brother, I was afraid he might mention I was there. Even though Antoine had other things on his mind, I imagined his surprise (and especially that of his parents) at hearing I'd come to spend a few days in Rosier without Hélène. Although I hadn't asked Patrice to keep quiet about my visit, I'm certain he never lies, so he was lying by omission by not mentioning I was there.

19

—

Marie-Aude and Jacques are the last people to whom I spoke about this book. Patrice's mourning doesn't intimidate me, but theirs does. I was afraid that my questions would revive their grief, which is absurd because their sorrow never sleeps and time will not soothe it. They combat this grief not by talking but by taking care of their granddaughters every chance they get, with great tact and attentiveness. Patrice, Étienne, Hélène, and I, all in our own ways, believe in the therapeutic virtues of talking. Jacques and Marie-Aude, like my parents, distrust words: "Never explain, never complain" could be their motto. So I waited until I'd almost finished this project before I even told them about it and then asked them to help by talking about what they are best equipped to recall: Juliette's first illness. Even between themselves, they don't speak of it, or of her second illness and her death, but in the hope that this book might one day help the girls, they accepted. When they began, they were sitting in armchairs in their living room, a good distance apart, but Jacques went over to sit next to his wife when she moved to the sofa, and he took her hand and held it all the way through. Whenever one of them spoke, the other watched with tender anxiety, fearing a collapse. Tears flowed; they regained control of themselves, apologized. It's their way of loving each other, and of carrying on with their lives.

Juliette was sixteen and beginning her next-to-last year at her lycée when she showed her mother a large, painful lump on her neck. She was taken immediately to the Hôpital Cochin in Paris, then to a radiology center where the diagnosis was Hodgkin's lymphoma, cancer of the lymphatic system. Jacques and Marie-Aude believe not in the unconscious but in the random activity of cells, so it would have been both useless and cruel to discuss the psychosomatic hypothesis with them, especially since in their daughter's case there isn't much to support it, although Patrice says that at the end of her life Juliette did speak a few times of a feeling of abandonment in her childhood. The more urgent question was about her treatment. Juliette's parents were extremely knowledgeable and very demanding, and their daughter's medical team found them difficult to deal with; in the end the doctor caring for her left the choice between radiation and chemotherapy up to them. Now they find it monstrous to have been made responsible for this decision and therefore burdened with a futile and tormenting regret: Had they chosen the other option, might the outcome have been different? Juliette had radiation, a less onerous treatment that did not make her hair fall out. After a few months, she was considered cured. She returned to dancing, school, took part in a fashion show. No more was said of her illness; not much had been said about it in the first place. Her brother, Antoine, fourteen at the time, never once heard the word *cancer*.

The following summer, in Brittany, she began to stumble and lose her balance. Usually so lively, she now seemed cranky, not at her best. In reality, she was trying to hide—and especially from herself—the fact that her legs were beginning to fail her. Her story is like Étienne's, except that her cancer did not return. The initial examinations were inconclusive; she had no less than three lumbar punctures, which must have been excruciating. Her parents feared she had multiple sclerosis. Finally, a neurologist at the Hôpital Cochin told them the truth: the problem was a lesion stemming from her radiation therapy. Though they'd tried to isolate the area of her back to be exposed to the ionizing radiation, two radiation fields had accidentally overlapped. Injury to the spinal cord in the overirradiated zone meant that nerve impulses had trouble reaching the legs, causing her increasing loss of control. But is there nothing you can do? asked the devastated parents. We can try to limit the damage, replied the neurologist, but his tone was not encouraging. Wait for the situation to stabilize. What's lost is gone; what we need to see now is how far this will go.

Neither Jacques nor Marie-Aude dared tell Juliette what the neurologist had said. They remained evasive, waited to be alone to break down in tears. Jacques kept remembering the day six months earlier when he'd accompanied Juliette to her treatment and, waiting behind the door, had heard the radiologists arguing about where to center the radiation on the grid traced on his daughter's back. He'd heard a loud voice, which had worried him, and, thinking back, he decided that was when the mistake must have been made. Because there had been a mistake, and it wasn't having chosen radiation over chemo. The radiation had definitely cured Juliette of her lymphoma, except they'd done it wrong and their negligence was costing his daughter her legs. Jacques and Marie-Aude laid siege to the radiology center, attempting to make the chief physician acknowledge his responsibility. He was, they recall, a cold and self-important man, both indifferent to their distress and disdainful of their scientific competence. He brushed away the Cochin neurologist's diagnosis, denied any malpractice, and ascribed Juliette's handicap—which it now clearly was—to a "hypersensitivity" to treatment for which no one was responsible, only nature. He practically said it was her own fault. Jacques and Marie-Aude hated that pedantic cold fish more than they'd ever hated anyone before, yet they vaguely realized that what they hated in him was their own helplessness. When they asked to see their daughter's medical file, the doctor sighed and promised to send it to them but never did. Later they were told it had disappeared.

And Juliette, all this time, what did she think? Hélène remembers she suffered from what the family called her "migraines," spending entire days lying on her bed in the dark. No one could talk to her or touch her; all sensory stimuli were becoming agonizing. Hélène also remembers something her mother once whispered to her: Juliette might wind up in a wheelchair, but she mustn't be told or she might stop fighting. Marie-Aude herself blurted out to me at one point that she didn't dare leave for work in the morning for fear that Juliette, in spite of all her courage, might "do something foolish." The atmosphere at home was infinitely worse than it had been the previous year. Hodgkin's lymphoma is a serious disease, but the survival rate is around 90 percent and although the danger had been real it had also been quickly contained, then eliminated. It had been a passing incident, whereas now they were sinking into catastrophe.

The word *irreversible* was taboo: Jacques and Marie-Aude

described that year as a constant battle, first to avoid saying the word, then to find the courage to say it. What they refused to tell their daughter, they first refused to admit to themselves. And then they had to. Juliette was about to come of age, and they began to understand the need to compile a dossier that would allow her to obtain financial assistance, a disabled person's card, a driver's license for a specially modified car, and other benefits that would now become part of her life. The dossier contained a declaration confirming the existence of a lesion, stabilized but permanent, in her spinal cord. The couple postponed as long as they could having to collect these documents, sign them, and hand them to Juliette, who signed them without comment. She received her disability card a few days before her eighteenth birthday.

At eighteen, this ravishing and athletic girl had to confront the fact that she would never walk unaided again. One of her legs would be partially paralyzed, the other one completely so. She would drag them along by leaning on crutches. She wouldn't be able to spread them when she made love for the first time. She would need help, the way she was helped to get out of the bathtub or go up stairs. One of the people who spoke at her funeral linked her vocation for justice to the injustice she had endured. When her parents had considered suing the radiology center, however, Juliette, who was already in law school, had opposed the idea. It was no more unjust to be left handicapped from the treatment than from the disease. It wasn't even particularly unjust. It was too bad, yes, unfortunate, but justice had nothing to do with it. To come to terms with her handicap, Juliette preferred to distance herself from its cause and those who might have been responsible for it.

Knowing her injury to be permanent, Juliette had a horror of being told gently, You never know, everything might come back.

With the best intentions in the world, Patrice's mother wanted to believe something would click into place one day and Juliette would walk again. An advocate of alternative medicine, she insisted that Juliette consult a spiritual healer for a laying on of hands, and the woman then showed Patrice how to massage Juliette's back: from top to bottom, for a long time, and when he reached the sacrum he was to shake his hands vigorously to disperse the bad energy. For several weeks Patrice conscientiously followed her instructions, expecting some improvement. As for Juliette, she loved being massaged, but for the pleasure of it, without any hope of being cured. She finally told him this and also told him she did not want to be trundled along mountain paths in a kind of sedan chair or taken to the beaches of the Landes and urged to roll around in the waves, as if that could do her any good. There were enough things that did help her, so why go through all that other folderol? Ingenious though they might be, she wasn't interested in contraptions that allowed someone who could not stand up to ski or climb Mont Blanc. That wasn't for her. Patrice understood and gave up all hope of one day seeing her walk again. He had never known her without crutches, and he loved her with them.

20

It's six in the evening in Étienne's office, a few months after he and Juliette met for the first time. Both have had a hard day. They ought to have gone straight home, he to Lyon, she to Rosier, but Juliette already knows that before closing up shop, Étienne likes to sit still for a moment in his armchair, his eyes closed. He's not necessarily thinking about his work that day or what the next one will bring—or if he is, it's not on purpose, and he doesn't dwell on those problems. He simply lets things go through his head, without passing judgment. That's when Juliette likes to join him, and although he used to prefer to be alone at such moments, now he awaits her visits with pleasure. They talk, or not; they have no trouble being silent together. As soon as she arrives this evening and sits down, propping her crutches against an arm of her chair, he can tell something's wrong. She says no, everything's fine. He

asks again. Eventually she tells him about an incident that afternoon. Incident, that's too strong a word: a tense moment, but it
affected her painfully. She'd asked a court usher to get some files
from her car, and he'd gone off with a sigh. That's all. He hadn't
said anything, merely sighed, but to Juliette that meant he found
having to do things for her because of her handicap irritating.
And yet, she says, I really try not to take advantage . . .

Étienne interrupts her: You're wrong. You should take more
advantage. Don't fall into that trap, don't drive yourself crazy
playing the cripple who's pretending not to be handicapped. You
need to get clear on this, decide that people owe you these little
services, and by the way they do owe them to you, and they're
usually happy to do them, happy because they're not in your position and because helping you reminds them just how happy they
are. You mustn't resent them for it—if you start that you'll never
see the end of it—but what I said is true.

Juliette smiles; she's often amused by his vehemence. They
could stop there but this evening he doesn't want to and asks,
You're fed up, aren't you?

She shrugs.

Me too, he adds, I'm fed up.

And when he describes this scene to me, he says again, I'm
fed up.

Then he explains: It's a simple but extremely important state-
ment, because it's something you can't let yourself say, can't even
let yourself think, insofar as that's possible. Because if you start
thinking "I'm fed up," that leads to "It's not fair" and "If only life
were different." Well, such thoughts are unbearable. If you start
thinking "It's not fair," you can't live anymore. If you start wishing life were different, that you could run like everyone else to
catch the métro or play tennis with your kids, then life becomes
poisoned. Such thoughts go nowhere, but they exist, and it's no

good spending all your energy trying to pretend they don't. But dealing with them—that's complicated.

With each other, Étienne and Juliette have some leeway, but the rule—and they note that they both follow it—is not to talk about these things with the others. By which they mean their others: Nathalie for him, Patrice for her. In theory, their spouses can hear everything, but it's important to hide these particular thoughts from them, because they cause pain, the pain of sorrow, helplessness, and guilt, which must not be passed on to them. But one must also be careful not to be too careful, not to police oneself too much with the other person. Sometimes, Étienne says, I let myself go with Nathalie. I blurt out that I'm sick of it, it's too hard and too unfair to have a plastic leg, it makes me want to cry, and I cry. This happens when the pressure's too great, every three or four years, then I'm good till the next time. What about you? You ever tell Patrice?

Now and then.

And you cry?

It happens.

While they're talking, tears start trickling down their cheeks, tears that flow freely, without shame, even with joy. Because being able to say "It's hard," "It's not fair," "I'm fed up" without worrying that your listener will feel guilty, being able to speak and be sure—these are Étienne's words—that the other person understands what you said as you meant it, nothing more, reading nothing else into it, is wonderful, a huge relief. So they keep talking. They know or sense that this sharing will happen only once, that they'll never allow this again, or else it would become an indulgence. But this evening they go for it.

Étienne says, What I do is, when I'm on the toilet, I keep score in a tennis game. I visualize the shots. I haven't played tennis in ten years but in my head I still play it and I know I'll miss it until the end.

For me, says Juliette eagerly, it's dancing. I loved dancing, I danced until I was seventeen, that's not very long, and at seventeen I knew it was over forever. Last month, when Patrice's brother got married, I watched the others dance and I wanted so much to join them I could have died. I was smiling, I love them, I was happy to be there, but then they played something that was popular when I had my legs, "Y.M.C.A."—you remember: *Why-Em-See-Ay!*—I think I'd have given ten years of my life to dance that, for the five minutes the song lasted . . .

Later, when they've made themselves almost giddy with these confessions, Juliette says, more seriously, At the same time, if that hadn't happened to me, I might not have met Patrice. Definitely not. Come to think of it, I would never have even noticed him. I'd have loved a completely different kind of man: more brilliant, masterful, my match in the marriage market because I was pretty and brilliant. I'm not saying my handicap made me a deeper person, but it's thanks to my legs that I'm with Patrice, thanks to them that the girls were born, and my girls chase away all bitterness and regret. Not a day goes by when I don't think, I have love. Everyone runs after it. Well, I can't run but I've got it. I love this life, I love my life, love it totally. You understand?

Oh yes, says Étienne. I love my life, too. That's why it's so hard to tell Nathalie when I'm fed up. Because if she hears that, she thinks I'd like a different life, and since she can't give me one she gets sad. But saying you're fed up doesn't mean you'd like some other life, or even that you're sad. You, are you sad?

Not anymore.

21

—

They had recognized each other. They'd known the same suffering, the kind one cannot understand without having gone through
it. They came from the same world. Their parents were middle-
class Parisians, scientists, Christians; Juliette's were right-wing,
Étienne's more to the left, but that difference paled next to the
lofty social position both families felt they enjoyed. Étienne and
Juliette had both married "beneath" themselves, as their parents
would have put it (Étienne's note: Not mine), and they'd married
for real love. Their marriages were the heart of their lives, the key
to their accomplishments. Étienne and Juliette were already sol-
idly grounded before they met and would have been surprised to
hear there was something missing from their lives. But when this
something appeared, they welcomed it with wonder and gratitude.
Étienne, true to his mania for contradiction, rejects the word

friendship, but I say that what they were together was friends and that having a true friend in life is as rare and precious as true love. Friendship between a man and a woman is more complicated, of course, because desire is involved and, with it, love. On that score, there's nothing to report, but Patrice and Nathalie both understood that for the first time someone else mattered in the lives of Juliette and Étienne, and they made their peace with that.

Aside from that one deeply personal talk in Étienne's office, they had hardly any private, intimate conversations. Their discussions were always about work. One can love working with someone the way one loves making love with someone, and Étienne says he'll always miss the pleasure of collaborating with Juliette. There was no physical contact between them. They shook hands when they first met, but not in parting that time in the office or ever again. They didn't embrace each other, either, or even nod in greeting, or say hello or good-bye. Whether they'd last been together the day before or just returned from a month's vacation, they'd meet as if one of them had been gone only a minute to fetch a dossier from the next room. But according to Étienne, there was something carnal and voluptuous in the way they practiced law together. They both lived for the moment when the flaw is discovered, when the logic clicks, unfolding on its own. I love it, Juliette would say, when your eyes start to shine. Their styles, as judges, could not have been more different. Juliette was composed, reassuring. She always began a hearing by explaining what would happen. What justice was, and why they were all there. The principle of proof, the importance of full debate. If she had to go over her explanations again, she did. She took all the time necessary, helped those who had trouble understanding or expressing themselves clearly. Étienne, on the other hand, was brusque and sometimes brutal, capable of cutting off a lawyer by announcing, I know you, Counselor. I know what you're going to say, there's no point in making your plea, next case. People left his hearings in a daze and left Juliette's feeling relieved. These differences persisted even in the style in which they rendered their judgments, Étienne told me, describing Juliette's writing as classic, clear, balanced, and his as more novelistic: rough, uneven, with sudden changes in tone that I, frankly, could never make out; my ear isn't experienced enough for that.

They fought the same battles, meaning Juliette was inspired by Étienne's crusades regarding housing law and especially consumer law, but I don't think they were driven by the same reasons. If someone as brilliant as Étienne chooses the *tribunal d'instance*, the provinces, petty cases, I think it's because he prefers to be at the top in his small arena rather than risk winding up even in second place in Paris. The Gospels, Lao Tzu, and the I Ching all urge us with one voice to "help the little people," but when people like Étienne or me, who are much alike in this respect, adopt such strategies of humility, it's obviously from a restless, thwarted taste for importance, and I detect in his enthusiasms a kind of possessive vanity, a desire to be recognized for accomplishments that to me seem slightly absurd—as if the literary vanity that grips me were spurred by something incomparably more noble.

Juliette did not have such problems. Obscurity suited her; she didn't mind that people took Étienne for her mentor and talked more about him than about her. Verdicts they had discussed at length but that were delivered by him appeared under his name in law journals. He offered several times to send some of her decisions to these journals, to put her in the spotlight, but she refused. I think what motivated her was both a disinterested love of justice and the unexpected satisfaction of being a judge after her husband's heart. The couple often discussed politics together, the way they discussed everything else, in fact, and although they agreed on the essentials, Patrice was so suspicious of all institutions, so quick to denigrate them whatever their merits, that Juliette found herself automatically on the side of order and continuity. She did feel she'd made great progress, however, with regard to her background: she voted socialist, or for the Greens when they weren't too much in the socialists' way, and read the articles Patrice recommended in the left-leaning *Politis* and *Monde diplomatique*. She'd been the one to introduce him to the popular aphorism that she'd learned at the ENM: the Penal Code is what keeps the poor from robbing the rich and the Civil Code is what lets the rich rob the poor. And she freely admitted there was a great deal of truth in the joke. In taking up her post at the *tribunal d'instance*, she'd expected to have to rubber-stamp more often than not the workings of an unjust social order, but thanks to Étienne, there she was at the forefront of a dangerous and exhilarating struggle to defend the widow and the orphan, the pauper against the prince. She rejected such rhetoric, of course, saying she was neither for nor against anyone, intent only on ensuring respect for the law, but increasingly, when the law journals talked about "the judge in Vienne," they meant two gimps instead of one.

At the time when Juliette replaced Jean-Pierre Rieux, jurisprudence was taking a harder line. Credit companies disgruntled over a few left-wing judges who systematically sided with their borrowers in default were filing appeals, sending the cases up to the Cour de cassation, the Supreme Court of Appeal. No less systematically, the Cour de cassation, which is by nature conservative, began to quash the *jugements en instance*. The unfortunates who'd rejoiced at having neither interest nor penalties to pay were learning that they did have to pay them after all, because a more powerful judge had rapped the knuckles of their sympathetic judge. To do this the Cour de cassation used two weapons and here, sorry, things must get a bit technical.

The first weapon is called the statute of limitations provision. The law says the creditor must take judicial action to enforce his rights within two years following the first payment received, or be thereafter barred from enforcing them, period. The idea is to keep a lending institution from suddenly demanding after ten years huge sums it has allowed to accumulate without ever attempting to bring the debtor to heel. This measure protects the borrower, obviously. What the Cour de cassation added here is a requirement that the statute be equitable, so that the same constraint must apply to both parties: the borrower, as well, thus has two years in which to contest the legality of his contract after signing it, and after two years, that's it, he has no more right to complain. Now, I don't know what a careful reader might think of this requirement, and I admit I might be too influenced by Étienne in my appreciation of these legal—and moral and political—issues, but I don't see how that statute can be called equitable, because it's still the creditor who sues the borrower, never the reverse. So all the creditor has to do is wait two years before attacking, serene in the knowledge that even if his contract is stuffed with abusive clauses, no one can say a word against it. To defend himself, the borrower would have had to *know* the contract was illegal upon signing it. He would have had to be *perfectly informed*, even though the spirit of the original law was to prevent any creditor from taking advantage of his ignorance.

For Étienne, Florès, and now Juliette, this trick of turning a clause intended to protect the borrower to the creditor's profit was a serious setback. Their judgments were based on law, but when it comes to interpreting the law, the Cour de cassation has the last word, and it was having it more and more often. The statute of limitations provision could not be trotted out every time, however, so the three judges still had a bit of room to maneuver. The situation turned critical when the Cour de cassation brought out its second weapon: a decree issued in the spring of 2000 stating that the judge is not automatically entitled (i.e., under his own initiative) to challenge any infractions of the law. That's classic free market thinking: the defendant cannot have more rights than the plaintiff; to right a wrong, the one who suffered it must make the complaint. In a lawsuit between a consumer and a credit industry professional, if the consumer does not complain about the contract, it's not for the judge to do that in his place. All this is fine in theory, but in reality the consumer doesn't complain, because he doesn't know the law, he's not the one who filed the lawsuit, and nine times out of ten he has no lawyer. Doesn't matter, says the Cour de cassation, the job of the judge is to do the judge's job: he should mind his own business, and if he's scandalized, he should keep it to himself.

Étienne, Florès, and Juliette were scandalized but hamstrung; the borrowers they'd plied with false hopes were dismayed. The credit companies rejoiced.

One October day in 2000, Étienne is in his office leafing through some law reviews. He comes across a commentated decision by the European Court of Justice, which he begins to read casually, then with increasing attention. The matter involves a consumer credit contract stipulating that any legal actions be brought before the court in Barcelona, where the credit company has its headquarters. So consumers who live in Madrid or Seville are required to travel to Barcelona to defend themselves? The clause is abusive, that's clear to the Barcelona judge, who denounces it. But in Spain as in France, the judge has no specific right to intervene, so he lays the matter before the European Court of Justice. The ECJ renders its verdict. Étienne reads the verdict. Even before he's finished, he gets up and hurries down to the ground floor, to the small room next to the larger courtroom where Juliette is presiding. Opening the connecting door, he beckons her. Juliette, like an actress summoned unexpectedly from the wings in the middle of a performance, tries to ignore him, but he's insistent. To the amazement of the court clerk, the usher, and the parties to a lawsuit over a defective human waste disposal unit, Juliette calls a recess, grabs her crutches, and hobbles into the little room where Étienne is waiting. What's going on? Read this. He hands her the law review. She reads:

"As to the question of whether a court seized of a dispute concerning a contract between a seller or supplier and a consumer may determine of its own motion whether a term of the contract is unfair, it should be noted that the system of protection introduced by the Directive is based on the idea that the consumer is in a weak position vis-à-vis the seller or supplier, as regards both his bargaining power and his level of knowledge . . . The aim of Article 6 of the Directive, which requires Member States to lay down that unfair terms are not binding on the consumer, would not be achieved if the consumer were himself obliged to raise the unfair nature of such terms . . . It follows that effective protection of the consumer may be attained only if the national court acknowledges that it has power to evaluate terms of this kind of its own motion."

Oof. In a film, gripping, dramatic music would accompany the heroine's discovery of that text. We'd see her lips moving softly as she reads; her face would express first puzzlement, then incredulity, and at last amazement. She would look up at the hero, stammering something like: But then . . . this means?

Reverse shot of him, calm, intense: Right.

I'm making fun just a little here and it's true, there is something comical in the contrast between that indigestible prose and
the joy it unleashed, but one could make fun this way of almost
any human endeavor in which one is not personally involved, and
so mock all commitments, all enthusiasm. Étienne and Juliette
have been fighting a battle the outcome of which will affect the
lives of tens of thousands of individuals. For months they've been
suffering one rout after another; they were about to admit defeat,
and now Étienne has discovered the crucial move that will change
the tide of battle. It's always delightful when a petty boss bullies
you, saying, That's the way it is, tough luck, I don't have to account
to anyone, and then you discover that above him is a bigger boss,
and this big boss says, You win. Not only does the ECJ contradict
the Cour de cassation, it outranks it, since European Union law
takes precedence over national law. Étienne knows nothing about
EU law, but already he finds it wonderful. And he begins to develop
the theory he expounded to us, I remember, on the morning of
Juliette's death: the higher the norm of law is set, the more generous
it is and the closer it gets to the great principles that inspire the
law. Rule by decree allows government to commit petty injustices, whereas the Constitution and the Declaration of the Rights
of Man dwell in the ethereal space of virtue—where they pro-
scribe such injustices. Fortunately, the Constitution and the Declaration of the Rights of Man are worth more than any decree. To
make one's creditor pay up is a right, that's understood, but there's
also a right to live a decent life, and when one has to choose
between them, the latter right can be said to spring from a higher
norm of law and so carries the day. It's the same for the landlord's
right to collect his rents and the tenant's right to a roof over his
head, and owing to the battles waged over the last ten years by
judges like Étienne and Juliette, that second right is becoming
"demurrable," which in practice means superior to the first.

So. Étienne gets excited, his eyes start to shine. Juliette has told him she loves it when his eyes shine. She loves and shares his exaltation, but in their partnership it's more or less her role to keep her feet on the ground, never to lose sight of the reality principle. And she tells him they have to think about this. Appealing to European Union law to counter national jurisprudence and enrage the Cour de cassation, well, you can always say it won't cost a thing, but that's not true, it might cost a great deal. Florès has been in contact with consumer associations that are engaged in protracted trench warfare with national jurisprudence on these matters. If the blitzkrieg Étienne and Juliette are busy planning were to fail, it might weaken that other long-term effort. Besides, if the ECJ tells them no, the credit companies will have a powerful new weapon to wield.

There follow feverish days of telephone calls and e-mails with Florès, and also with a professor of EU law, Bernadette Le Baut-Ferrarese, who when consulted becomes passionately interested in the question. She feels the response of the ECJ is impossible to predict but an appeal is worth a try, always remembering that it's like a presidential pardon in the days of the death penalty: double or nothing, the last card they can play. In the end, they decide to try. Who will make the trip? Who'll write the *jugement provocateur*? Any one of the three judges could have taken on the job, but it seems this is a foregone conclusion: Étienne is the one who most loves going to the front lines.

For a few months now, dossiers have been piling up on his desk relating to an unsecured loan contract offered by our old friend Cofidis and catchily named Libravou, meaning, "It's Up to You." The Libravou contract could be studied in schools as a perfect example of a near swindle. It's presented as a "no-fee application for a cash account," with the words NO FEE printed in a large font size, while the interest rate appears in teeny-tiny letters on the back of the offer and it's 17.92 percent, which when increased by late penalties crosses the line into usury. In the pile, Étienne chooses at random the dossier into which he will slip his little bomb: *Cofidis SA v. Jean-Louis Fredout.* It's not a big deal: Cofidis demands 16,310 francs, 11,398 of which are capital, the rest interest and penalties. At the hearing, M. Fredout is absent and has no lawyer. The one Cofidis has, on the other hand, is a veteran of the Vienne bar, an old hand who doesn't grow alarmed when Étienne points out that "the financial clauses are difficult to read," that "this lack of legibility is in contrast with the particularly noticeable mention of the no-fee offer," and that "the financial clauses may thus be considered abusive." The lawyer isn't worried, he knows all Étienne's quibbles by heart and anyway he respects him, and in a facetious but not at all aggressive tone, as if they were putting on a well-rehearsed fencing match, he replies that, even if the clauses are abusive, who cares, because the contract dates from January 1998, the suit was filed in August 2000, the statute of limitations has definitely expired, so sorry, Monsieur le Président, nice try but the law is the law, and let's leave it at that.

Fine, says Étienne, let's. Decision in two months. The humbler he seems, the more tickled he is inside. If it were up to him, he'd deliver his ruling next week, but everything has to seem normal, including the usual delay. The hearing concludes at six on Friday afternoon and Saturday morning he's at his computer at home. He writes in excitement and pleasure, often laughing aloud. In two hours, he's done: the decision is fourteen pages, unusually long. He calls up Juliette to read it to her, and she laughs gleefully as well. Then he phones Florès and Bernadette, who's now a full member of the conspiracy. They take their time, verify everything, consider and reconsider every word. The details are quite technical, of course, but the idea can be simply stated. Étienne's ruling will find for Fredout but maintain that he can't hand down a definitive decision because the law is not clear, and to clarify it he must ask the ECJ a question, which is called a prejudicial question. Here's the question: Is it consistent with the European Community directive that the national judge may not as a matter of course determine that a clause in a contract is abusive even after the statute of limitations has expired? Give me a yes or no answer, and I will rule accordingly.

This done, the conspirators bite their nails for the requisite two months, after which they send to the plaintiff, the defendant, and above all to the ECJ copies of the decision that isn't really one because it will hinge on the answer to Étienne's prejudicial question. Shortly afterward, Étienne runs into the Cofidis lawyer, who's a bit disconcerted by this unidentified legal object. But that's fine, he jokes, whatever amuses you . . . We're going to lodge an appeal with the Cour de cassation, which will do its job, and by annulling the decision it will annul your question. We'll only have lost a year, I couldn't care less, you too, so it's just your guy who'll cherish fond hopes and in the end he'll pay up all the same. Étienne has seen this coming and smiles. I don't think, he says, that things will go like that. The Cour de cassation itself says that only appeals based on the main issue of a suit may be heard, which excludes decisions still under advisement, and what you've received is a decision under advisement. The other man raises his eyebrows. You're sure? Absolutely, replies Étienne.

Oh.

* * *

The gears start turning. In Luxembourg, they begin by having Étienne's question translated into all the European languages and sent off to all the member states. Everyone's free to weigh in. Six months go by. One April morning in 2001 a thick envelope from the ECJ arrives at the *tribunal d'instance*. Étienne is alone in his office but he does the impossible: he waits for Juliette before opening it. They ask not to be disturbed. The envelope contains two documents, one very thick—a report from Cofidis—and the other short: it's an opinion from the European Commission, one of the important institutions—like the ECJ—of the European Union. Étienne and Juliette basically know what's in the long document, so all the suspense hangs on the other one and that's why, to enjoy this delicious suspenseful torment, they force themselves to read the Cofidis report first. Twenty-seven densely written pages, concocted by a squad of lawyers in crisis mode. The enemy has smelled danger and brought out the heavy artillery. The preamble immediately speaks of "an unproductive atmosphere of rebellion," and "the revolt sparked by certain judges backed by certain unions, and even by certain members of the Syndicat de la Magistrature." You see, observes Étienne, delighted, they always write the same way, the reactionaries, no matter what century we're in. Next, in order of combat, come the properly judicial arguments—I'll spare you the details—in support of the main argument, which is political: if we keep harassing credit companies and favoring borrowers in default, the entire system will take a body blow and it's the honest borrower who will suffer the consequences. In short, nothing unexpected, aside from the vehement tone. In a different context this stuff would appear benign; as judicial prose, it's a personal attack, with a bazooka. That's flattering, exciting. Juliette and Étienne have read every line of the report. Now for the verdict. The European Commission is not the ECJ, it delivers an opinion, not a decision, but that opinion is generally followed and if the commission says no, the ECJ will surely say no as well. A no would mean defeat, humiliation. Étienne and Juliette would have to bear that failure; they're not going to commit seppuku in the office, but they know they'd be devastated. You read first, says Étienne, you're tougher than I am. Juliette starts reading. Principle of effectiveness . . . compensation by the judge for the ignorance of one of the parties . . . reference to the Barcelona decree . . .

She looks up with a smile: It's yes.

It's as if we were on a wooden bridge, says Étienne. A shaky, dangerous bridge. We've put one foot on it. So far, so good. Now we step out with the other.

(As I write this, I realize how bold this simile is for a one-legged man.)

Étienne doesn't wait for the ECJ to confirm the commission's opinion: he ups the ante by asking a second prejudicial question, which also concerns the judge's right to challenge an injustice about which the victim has not complained, but this time Étienne tackles it from another direction. A certain M. Giner replaces M. Fredout, and the ACEA (European Automobile Manufacturers Association) replaces Cofidis, but aside from that the case is practically the same. At the hearing, Étienne observes that the overall effective rate, the TEG (*taux effectif global*), is not mentioned in the credit offer, which he considers irregular. No one there except Juliette is aware of the success of his first raid or suspects he is planning another. The ACEA lawyer therefore confidently offers the argument he'd prepared if the quibbler, as expected, quibbled. The nature of the irregularity, if there is one, springs from "protective public order," which is outside the judge's jurisdiction.

Protective public order, that's another innovation by the Cour de cassation, which since the 1970s has distinguished it from "directive public order." Protective public order concerns only the individual, not society. In such cases, it is up to the individual to assert his rights and the judge, who represents society, thus has no cause to take an interest there as a matter of course. Directive public order, that's something else: it concerns the general interest and especially the organization of the market. Its violation thus can and must be challenged by the judge.

Étienne finds this distinction pathetic. I handled penal cases up north, he says, and I'm handling them again in Lyon now. It's in the name of public order that I agree to perform the extremely unpleasant duty of locking people up. It's in the name of public order that I agree to throw in prison thugs who've stolen car radios. Justice is a violent thing. I accept that violence, but on the condition that the order it serves be coherent and indivisible. The Cour de cassation says that in protecting M. Fredout and M. Giner we are only advocating on behalf of individuals who ought to be clever enough to protect themselves on their own, or too bad for them. I don't agree. I feel that in protecting M. Fredout and M. Giner I protect all of society. In my estimation there is only a single public order.

One of the advantages of EU law, continues Étienne, is that it doesn't just lay down rules, it also sets out the intention behind each rule, and one is therefore justified in invoking this intention. The intention behind the EU directive on the TEG was perfectly clear, and perfectly free market: to organize free competition in the credit market. That's why the directive required that all contracts in Europe mention the TEG: so that competition would take place in complete transparency. Omitting said mention is an irregularity, there is no dispute about that, but here's the thing: the Cour de cassation forbids me to challenge this irregularity, on the grounds that in so doing I'm dealing only with people (protective public order) *and not the market* (directive public order). So I'm asking the ECJ: Is the mention of the TEG there to protect the borrower or to organize the market? Since the directive *plainly spells out* "to organize the market," my question is in fact even simpler: *Did I read correctly?* If I did read the directive correctly, Étienne concludes, the jurisprudence of the Cour de cassation makes no sense.

In hindsight, Étienne finds his Fredout brief poorly written and even a bit specious. The ECJ, in his opinion, could have rejected it, and he suspects it was approved for the wrong reasons: because the court did not want to miss a golden chance to assert its preeminence over national law. Étienne is very proud of the Giner decision, however. As a legal object, it delights him. First because it is not a left-wing decision. Étienne does not see himself at all as the dangerous leftist denounced by the Cofidis lawyers. He describes himself as a social democrat but believes in the virtues of competition, so it's all the more exhilarating to trip up an ultra free market consumer credit company with its own logic, with an argument that would please a captain of industry. Above all, Étienne loves the style of the Giner decision, the contrast between the vast scope of the problem—what is public order?—and the deceptively naïve, Socratic, and confounding question that resolves it: Did I read correctly? He likes that simple and obvious way to hit the bull's-eye. I understand him. That's what I like in my work, too: when it's simple, obvious, when it gets things right. And of course, when it's effective.

Effectiveness: let's talk about that. Before he left his post in Vienne, Étienne was able to deliver a judgment to forfeit all interest claimed by Cofidis in the Fredout case. In the Giner case, the creditor, sensing a change in the wind, preferred to drop the suit. After this double victory and above all the fact that it created jurisprudence, Juliette and Étienne were "insulted in the *Dalloz*," France's most prestigious legal journal, by law professors who described "the judge in Vienne" as a kind of public enemy number one. And that was a point of pride with them. As a result of their campaign, the law on the statute of limitations provision was changed, the duties of a judge were expanded, and the debts of tens of thousands of poor people were alleviated, entirely legally. That's not as spectacular as, say, abolishing the death penalty but is enough for Étienne and Juliette to tell themselves that they did some good, and even that they were great judges.

22

―

Étienne says he had himself transferred to Lyon as an examining judge because after eight years at the *tribunal d'instance* he was exhausted, and besides, he had to leave someday, so it might as well be with a victory. The lawyers of Vienne insinuate behind his back that his transfer was a punishment: he was pissing everyone off and the Ministry of Justice was tired of him. Either way, he readily admits his new job wasn't a promotion, that Vienne was the position of a lifetime, and while he may have more prestigious posts later on, he doubts he'll have a more exciting one.

Leaving that position meant leaving Juliette as well. Lyon is only a half-hour drive from Vienne, but they both knew that what kept their friendship alive was the daily companionship, the cases they both discussed, the opportunity to pop into each other's offices at any moment and live together at work the way other couples live at home. After he moved, they had lunch a few times, the two families spent a few Sundays together, but the occasions were so clearly not the same that they didn't keep that up. In the end, it didn't matter; Étienne felt that Juliette had become so much a part of him that in his mind she was the voice of authority to whom he addressed part of his interior monologue, and he was sure it was the same for her. They phoned each other occasionally. She kept him up to date on court news, the gossip about the clerks and ushers, which he enjoyed the way children do when they day-dream about being dead and listening to the chatter at their funerals. Juliette wasn't getting along as well with his replacement, another woman, but that was normal; she and Étienne had shared something extraordinary, and such things rarely last forever. The exhilaration that had carried her through their five years of fight-ing against the credit companies and the Cour de cassation had subsided, leaving her tired. She worked incredible hours to keep up with her cases, going to bed at midnight, rising at five, always afraid of falling behind and never catching up. Listening to her, he could tell she was losing ground and he would have liked to be there to help her as he once had, turning even the dullest work into a satisfying challenge. He was relieved when she announced she was pregnant: now, at least, she'd have to take a break. But this pregnancy was harder than the first two. She was the one who'd decided to have a third child; Patrice had been somewhat reluctant, but she'd insisted, and it would be their last. Diane was born March 1, 2004. Étienne saw Juliette in the maternity ward, then at Rosier, with the newborn. While Amélie and Clara played at mothering their little sister, Juliette gazed intently at her three daughters, and in her eyes Étienne saw love, of course, and happi-ness, but something else as well that he couldn't or wouldn't iden-tify, and it tore at his heart. She returned to work at the end of the August holidays; it was her second "back to court" at summer's end without him. When they spoke on the phone, the words *fatigue*, *weakness, exhaustion* kept coming up, soon to be joined by *dread*, which he'd never heard her say before.

One December morning, Patrice awoke to the sound of labored breathing: next to him, Juliette was weeping and choking. He tried to calm her. Between spasms, she gasped out that she didn't know what was happening to her but felt it was serious. Patrice made an emergency appointment with an internist in Vienne, and since it was Saturday and the girls wouldn't be in school or with their nanny, the whole family had to go. During the consultation, Amélie and Clara drew pictures in the waiting room. The doctor sent Juliette to have an emergency chest X-ray. To distract his increasingly restless daughters, Patrice took them to a bookstore, where the girls soon wreaked havoc on a shelf of children's books. With Diane wailing in his arms, Patrice patiently reshelved the books in his daughters' wake, apologizing to the store clerk, who fortunately had children of her own and understood completely. Father and daughters returned to the radiologist's office and, armed with the X-ray, they all went back to the internist, who seemed concerned and sent them on to Lyon for a different scan. They drove off, but they'd spent all morning with the doctors and the girls hadn't had lunch or a nap, Diane needed changing, all three were screaming away in the backseat, and Juliette in the front was in no condition to soothe them. It was hell. They waited again at the hospital in Lyon for the scan, but luckily there was a playroom for children, with a pool full of balloons. Every ten minutes an elderly lady asked Patrice where she was and he said, In the hospital, in Lyon, in France. He was so overwhelmed that he hadn't had time to be worried but when the diagnosis arrived—a pulmonary embolism—he was surprised to feel relieved. A pulmonary embolism is serious, but it isn't cancer. Juliette was sent by ambulance to the Clinique Protestante de Fourvière in Lyon and there put on intravenous anticoagulants to dissolve the blood clots blocking her lungs. Patrice took the girls home, then returned with some clothes and toiletries for Juliette, who'd be spending a few days in the clinic. Before leaving, Patrice saw the doctor, who said the scan showed nothing alarming. The only slight problem was that the radiation seventeen years earlier seemed to have left traces of fibrosis in the lungs, and it was difficult to distinguish between old lesions and any new ones, but on the whole, everything was under control.

As soon as Juliette was admitted to the clinic, she called Étienne. He remembers her words: Come, come right away, I'm scared. And when he entered her room half an hour later: I'm worse than scared, I'm terrified.

What's terrifying you?

She waved vaguely at the tube connected to the intravenous bag hanging on its little gallows: That. Being sick again. Gasping for air. Choking to death.

Her voice was jagged, angry, fierce with a revolt he'd never seen in her before. That wasn't her style, revolt; neither was bitterness or sarcasm, but that day he saw her in biting, sharp-tongued rebellion. Her face, which even in the greatest fatigue did not usually look harsh, was stern and even hostile. With a tight little smile that seemed even more alien to her, she said, I'd been wondering lately if I ought to buy more retirement insurance, but I'll save myself the trouble. Why bother?

Without taking the bait, Étienne calmly asked if she'd been told she was going to die, and she had to say no. She'd been told the same as Patrice: pulmonary embolism, perhaps due to the

radiation therapy, which made her so *fucking* mad—and that was
a word she never used, but that day, yes: it made her fucking mad
to be still paying for an old illness she'd thought long gone.

After a pause, she spoke again, more quietly: I'm horribly afraid
of dying, Étienne. You know, when I was sixteen and got sick I
had a romantic idea about death. I found it seductive, and although
I didn't know if I was really in danger, I was up for it. You, too—
you told me one day that at eighteen you thought, cancer . . . that
could be cool. I remember very well: you said "cool." But now,
with the girls, I'm appalled. The idea of leaving them horrifies
me. You understand?

Étienne nodded. He understood, of course, but instead of saying what anyone else would have told her ("Who's talking about
dying? You've got a pulmonary embolism, not cancer, don't be so
frightened!"), he said, If you die, the girls aren't going to die of that.

They will, they need me too much. No one will ever love them
as I do.

How do you know? You're going a bit far. I hope you're not
about to die, but if you are, you have work to do. You've got to tell
yourself this and really believe it: *Their lives will not end with me.
They can be happy even without me.* It's hard but that's what you
have to do.

When Patrice returned after leaving the children with neighbors,
Juliette didn't let him see any sign of the panic Étienne had witnessed. She played the role of the model patient, confident and
upbeat, and she stayed that way almost till the end. The doctors
said the crisis had passed; there wasn't any reason not to believe
them, and perhaps she did. She went home after five days with a
prescription for some support hose and anticoagulants meant to
prevent further clots and restore normal pulmonary function.

She never got it back. She was always breathless, gasping like a fish out of water, craning her neck, with a constant weight on her chest. Is it unbearable? asked the doctor over the phone. Unbearable, no, since she was bearing it, but distressing and, even more, frightening. Wait a little while for the medications to take effect. Let's see where we are in January.

Over the Christmas holidays, which the family spent with Patrice's parents in Savoie, her daughters constantly complained that she was tired all the time, hadn't decorated the tree, wasn't doing anything with them. So she'd pretend, joke around, play the game of the worn-out old mama who needs to be tossed in the trash, which made the girls laugh and shriek, No, no! Not the trash! To Patrice, though, she confided that that's exactly how she felt: damaged, beyond repair, ready for the rubbish heap. The house was bustling with lots of people, noise, and cavalcades of children up and down the stairs. The couple took refuge in their room as much as possible, lying on the bed in each other's arms, and she would murmur, stroking his cheek, My poor dear, you drew an unlucky number, and Patrice would tell her he'd picked a real winner, the best in the world. Touched by his utter sincerity, she'd say, I'm the one who picked the winner. I love you.

Boxing Day was also the day of the tsunami. The family learned that Hélène and Rodrigue were safe even before learning what had happened, after which they didn't miss a single newscast or any of the special reports that allowed viewers to follow the catastrophe live, minute by minute. Those devastated tropical beaches, the straw huts, the people in rags who wailed and wept, all seemed unbelievably far from snowy Savoie, from the compact stone house, the blaze in the fireplace. They threw on another log, felt sorry for the victims, enjoyed feeling safe. Juliette did not feel safe, not at all. Everyone was treating her as a convalescent rather than an invalid, acting as if she were better, but she knew she wasn't, because it wasn't normal to be always short of breath. She could see that Patrice was worried, and she didn't want to add to his anxiety. I imagine that she wanted to call Étienne and that if she didn't, it wasn't to spare him the worry (*him* she knew she could worry as much as she wanted), but because calling Étienne was like taking an extremely powerful and efficacious drug, one to be kept in reserve for truly great need. She was already in bad shape, but she was beginning to suspect that soon she would be much worse.

The day after their return to Rosier, Patrice had to take her back to the hospital, where a complication of the embolism was diagnosed: water in the pleura, the thin membrane around the lungs and inner walls of the chest cavity, was compressing her breathing. She spent New Year's in the hospital in Vienne, where they drained the liquid from her lungs, then let her go home again, telling her that now she should feel better. Again, days passed and she didn't feel better. Again, she was hospitalized, this time in the pneumonia ward at the Hôpital Lyon-Sud. Again, the doctors drained her lungs, but this time they analyzed the liquid from the pleura, where they found metastatic cells, and told her that once again she had cancer.

23

—

That morning Étienne had accompanied Timothé, his eldest son, to his tennis lesson. Sitting on a bench behind the chain-link fence, he was watching him play when his cell phone rang. Juliette said what she had to say, straight out. Her voice did not quaver; she was calm, nothing like the time she'd called in anguish from the Clinique Protestante a month earlier. Étienne was profoundly calm as well, anchoring himself the way he knows how to do, deep in his solar plexus. He considered rushing immediately to Lyon-Sud but decided to wait, because he was working that day, because she'd told him that Patrice was there, because he preferred to see her alone, and because he knew from experience that the evening is the most difficult time in a hospital room, and also the moment of greatest intimacy.

He arrived after dinner. She watched him walk up to the foot of the bed, but no farther. No bending over her, kissing her, squeezing her shoulder or hand. He knew that all day long she had been able to let herself go in Patrice's arms, listening to him murmur to her the tender, silly, soothing words one tells a little girl awakened in the dark by a nightmare: Don't be afraid, I'm here, take my hand, squeeze my hand, as long as you hold on to my hand nothing bad will happen to you. With Patrice, she could be a little girl: he was her man. With him, Étienne, it was something else, and she was a different woman, a capable person in charge of her life and fighting for it. Patrice was her solace, not Étienne. But she had to take care of Patrice, not Étienne. She had to have courage for Patrice, whereas with Étienne she had a right to feel what one denies oneself with those one loves: terror and despair.

She seemed as calm as she had been on the phone that morning. They were both silent for a moment; then she said it wasn't lung cancer she had but breast cancer. The primary tumor was in the breast; the lung trouble was a metastasis. They'd given her a bone scan that afternoon to see if the cancer had also spread there, but the results were inconclusive, or perhaps they simply hadn't dared tell her what they'd found. In any case, it was bad.

Étienne recalled something he'd read in a book by the oncologist Laurent Schwartz: the cancerous cell is the only living thing that is immortal. Étienne thought: She's thirty-three years old. Instead of sitting in the armchair near the bed, he perched himself gingerly as far from her as he could get, on the cover of the enormous cast-iron radiator, which diffused a stifling heat throughout the room. Since she said nothing more, he spoke. He told her that from now on things would change every day: treatments, protocols, hopes, false hopes—that's what is hardest about an illness like this and she'd have to prepare herself. He told her to restrict as much as possible visits from well-meaning people who just eat up your energy. He told her the essential thing was to hang on, day after day. To conserve her strength. For example, working in Vienne—that was too hard, she'd done enough. If she was well enough in a few months to consider going back to work, she should ask for a transfer to Lyon, as he had. He was quite bossy on that point, even offering to write her a letter and speak to the chief justice of the court of appeal in Grenoble about it. He did not mention her girls again, said no more about preparing herself to leave them or preparing them for what was coming. He knew that's what she was thinking about but for the moment he had nothing to add to what he had already said at the Clinique Protestante, and he fell silent.

There was another pause. Then Juliette said she didn't want to be dispossessed of her illness the way she'd been when she was sixteen. Her parents had devoted all their love, all their energy, all their knowledge to protecting her; if they could have, they would have had the cancer for her, but she no longer wanted anyone to have it instead of her. She wanted to experience it fully, even unto death if death was what was waiting for her now, which seemed likely, and she was counting on Étienne to help her.

Do you remember, he asked her, the first night of your illness, the first time? The night of the day they told you you had a cancer?

No, Juliette did not remember. She didn't remember having heard those words: You have cancer. And she didn't remember having understood, after the fact, that what she'd had had been cancer. It must have happened, obviously, since she did know it, but the moment when she passed from ignorance or confusion into knowing that, the moment when that word was spoken . . . escaped her. You understand what I mean about being dispossessed of my illness?

Fine, said Étienne. So this will be your first night. And I'm going to talk to you about mine. It's important.

* * *

I've already related how at the end of our first family meeting with Étienne, after two hours of monologue from which I emerged feeling as if my brain had been centrifuged, he turned to me and said, You ought to think over what I said about the first night. Perhaps it's something for you. I did think about it—and began to write this book. He returned to the subject at our initial private discussion, when I wrote down as precisely as I could his story of that night in the Institut Curie, with the rat eating at him and the mysterious words that saved him in the morning. I didn't understand much of it but thought, yes, it's important, and we'll come back to it sooner or later, so maybe I'll see things clearer then. And here we are, three months later, still in his kitchen sitting at the little table with our espressos, as he tells me about his visit to Juliette the day she learned she had cancer. He tells me again what he said to her; he tells the same story of that first night. I listen avidly, but the phrase that saved him is still elusive. I take notes. The next day I look in my earlier notebook for what I'd written that other time, and my notes are identical. Word for word, they're the same disappointing phrases, without any of the oracular illumination that made, he says, the *real* words so splendid. Discouraged, I decide that the only way to talk about this moment is to have experienced it—and that words fail even Étienne whenever he describes his own experience. Leafing through the notebook, I come across a quotation from *Mars*, which I'd been rereading at the time: "As we know, the cancerous tumors themselves don't hurt; what hurts are the healthy organs being compressed by the tumors. I believe the same thing applies to soul sickness: *Wherever it hurts, is me.*" I go back to Étienne's words. For example: "My disease is part of me. It is me. So I cannot hate it." The thoughts are similar but not exactly the same. And Fritz

Zorn drives the point home: "My parents' legacy in me is like a gigantic cancerous tumor: everything that suffers in me, my anguish, my torment, my despair, is me." Étienne doesn't say that, he doesn't say that a family or social neurosis has taken the form of a tumor to weigh on his soul, but he says and repeats in every way: My disease is me. It is not outside me. Well, what he's saying, or in any case what something or someone deep inside him is saying, is the opposite of what he says out loud in the light of day. *Then* he says, like Susan Sontag in her lovely and dignified essay *Illness as Metaphor*, that the psychological explanation of cancer is both a myth without any scientific foundation and wickedly immoral, because it "culpabilizes" the patient. What Étienne says in the shadows, however, is what Fritz Zorn and Pierre Cazenave say, that his cancer is not a foreign aggressor but a part of him, an intimate enemy that may not even be an enemy. The first way of thinking is rational; the second is magical. One can claim that growing up, which psychoanalysis is supposed to help us do, means abandoning magical thinking for rational thinking, yet one can also maintain that nothing should be abandoned, that what is true on one floor of the mind may not be true on another, but that one must live on every floor of the mind, from the cellar to the attic. I think that's what Étienne does.

Before leaving Juliette, Étienne said, I don't know what will happen tonight, but something will. Tomorrow you'll be different. When he returned the following evening at the same time, Juliette's face was full of dismay. It didn't work, she said. I didn't manage to make the kind of conversion you described. I can't see the disease the way you do, in fact I don't really understand how you see it. With me, it's ridiculous—I see it over there, like something lying in wait for me in that armchair.

She pointed to the imitation leather chair with its metal tubing framework, passed up once again by Étienne in favor of the radiator.

(Reading this page three years later, Étienne said that the thing huddled watchfully in the chair had reminded him of my fox on François Roustang's couch. Me, I think what Juliette said that day was the opposite of what Étienne says. She was telling him, My disease is outside me. It's killing me, but it isn't me. And I also think she never saw it any other way.)

Well, you've been through your first night, said Étienne. You're beginning your relationship with illness. You gave it some room, but not all the room. And that's fine.

Juliette did not seem convinced. She sighed, like someone who's failed an exam and prefers to drop the subject. Then she said sadly, My girls won't remember me.

You don't remember your mother either from when you were little, Étienne replied. Nor do I mine. We don't see the faces they had anymore. And yet, they live on inside us.

He remembers those words, which he says simply came to him. And without thinking either, I tell him, You talked a lot to me about your father but not your mother. Tell me about her. He looks at me, a little surprised; there's a pause—nothing's coming to mind, evidently—and then he's off. He describes her lonely childhood in Jerusalem, where her grandfather ran the French hospital. The little girl didn't attend school; her mother taught her at home. For a long time all she knew of the world was her anxious and limited family circle. Étienne's father, too, was raised in great solitude, and then the two solitudes met each other. Étienne's mother loved that eccentric, stubborn, unhappy man with everything she had. She managed to protect their children from his depression, to pass on to them a freedom and an aptitude for happiness neither she nor her husband possessed, and Étienne admires her for that. He was the third child. Before his birth, the second child, Jean-Pierre, had died at the age of one from respiratory distress. He had been taken to the hospital, where he suffocated in atrocious and incomprehensible suffering far from his mother, who had been forbidden to stay with him and who for the rest of her life never forgot that her baby had died alone, without her. That, says Étienne, is what I can tell you about my mother.

Juliette asked the doctors at Lyon-Sud to be frank with her, and they were. They told her she would not get better and would die of her cancer; they could not predict how much time she had left, but in theory it might be years. She should expect those years to be very difficult, with constant treatments and a deteriorating quality of life. But Juliette meant to make the most of things, she had a husband and three daughters to be with as long as possible, and she decided to submit to the treatments patiently. A week after her diagnosis, she began chemotherapy and Herceptin, administered once a week at the hospital. That was for the cancer. As for the respiratory problems, the anticoagulants had unfortunately already proved their uselessness. Her lungs were wrecked, "cardboard," the radiologist had said, shaking his head sadly. He'd never seen a woman her age in such bad shape. They had no choice but to put her on oxygen. So two enormous tanks of oxygen were delivered to Rosier, trundled from the van to the house on a trolley, one for the bedroom, the other for the living room. There was a valve to regulate the flow of oxygen through a long tube that ended in a nasal cannula, a loop anchored behind the ears and fitted with two soft hollow prongs that tucked into the nostrils. Whenever she felt breathless, Juliette would wear the device and get some relief. Everyone vaguely hoped that this assistance would prove temporary, that the anticancer treatments would help on this front as well, but instead Juliette needed more and more oxygen. Toward the end she wore the device almost all the time and was saddened to think that her daughters would remember her as an invalid or some creature out of science fiction.

When Amélie asked her, Mama, are you going to die? Juliette chose to be as frank as the doctors had been with her. Yes, she replied, everyone dies one day. Even Clara, Diane, and you will die, but only in a very, very long time, and Papa as well. My death isn't very, very far away, but at least it's a little far away.

In how much time?

The doctors don't know, but not right away. I promise, not right away. So don't be afraid.

Amélie and Clara were afraid, naturally, but less, I think, than if they'd been lied to. And in a way, these frank words reassured not only the two little girls, allowing them to keep living their little-girl lives, but also their father. Patrice lives in the present. What sages throughout history have proclaimed the secret of happiness, being here and now, without regretting the past or worrying about the future, is something he practices naturally. We all know in theory that it's useless to agonize over problems that might arise five years down the road, because we have no idea if they'll still be the same problems in five years or even if we'll be around to deal with them. We know this, but it doesn't stop us from fretting. Patrice doesn't fret. His carefree attitude goes along with candor, trust, renunciation, all the virtues praised in the Beatitudes, and I suspect that what I'm writing here will puzzle him because his anticlerical culture is so intransigent, whereas I'm surprised that fervent Christians like his in-laws don't recognize this confirmed secularist's attitude toward life as simply the spirit of the Gospels. Like a child snug in bed repeating a magic formula that soothes him, Patrice kept repeating, like his daughters, Not right away. In three, four, five years. During those three, four, five years Juliette would grow ever more fragile and dependent; his task would be to care for her, help her, carry her the way he had from the beginning. I don't mean to paint an idyllic picture; Patrice was beaten down by anguish and insomnia like anyone else, but I believe—because he told me so—that he quickly put this program in place: to be there, to carry Juliette, to live the time allotted to them together while ignoring as much as possible the moment it would end. And he says that carrying out this program helped them all—him, her, and their girls—immeasurably.

Hearing of Juliette's illness, Patrice's mother produced out of nowhere an unorthodox medical researcher named Beljanski, whose plant-based compounds were said to have cured (not just helped, cured) patients with cancer and AIDS. Unconvinced by the supportive material she cited, only half believing—if that—her claims, but reluctant to rule anything out, Patrice tried to convince Juliette to bolster her chemotherapy with these compounds, which their family doctor could procure for her. Ever her parents' daughter, Juliette told him that if there were a miracle pill for cancer or AIDS, the world would know it. Ever his parents' son, Patrice explained that it would be more widely known if Beljanski's discoveries didn't threaten the vested interests of drug companies, which were in league against him. This kind of talk exasperated Juliette, and they'd often argued about it. She couldn't stand the conspiracy theories he openly admitted favoring, and although he beat a retreat, he did not give up. Even if she didn't believe in the pills, he asked her to try them *for him*, so that if she died he would not reproach himself for neglecting even the tiniest chance to save her. She sighed. If it will help you feel better, that's different, all right. Their doctor arrived with the capsules, explained the instructions, and when she finally gave in, although concerned that the treatment might counteract the effect of the Herceptin, the doctor simply shrugged and said it was a dietary supplement that wouldn't do any harm even if it didn't do any good. Juliette went along all the more reluctantly in that she didn't dare admit to her oncologists what she was doing. When she stopped taking the capsules after a few weeks, Patrice hadn't the heart to argue with her.

She was exhausted, sleeping poorly, and hardly an hour went by during the day when she didn't need her oxygen. None of the little miseries that attend a serious illness gave her a pass: an allergy to the portacath, the device inserted beneath the skin to facilitate injections and chemo; a thrombosis that turned her arm purple up to the shoulder and sent her back to the emergency room. The doctors did feel, however, that she was doing well with the chemotherapy—better than she'd feared and better than Étienne (remembering his own) had thought she would do. It was encouraging. Patrice even began to wonder if it might work after all. What if the doctors, honestly wishing to avoid encouraging hopes that might be crushed, had been too pessimistic? What if she were cured? What if she at least had a long remission, without too many treatments, too much suffering? They could do things once the nice weather returned: walks in the forest, picnics . . .

There was a kind of respite in February, which was why Juliette allowed Hélène, Rodrigue, and me to come visit, with the wig in our luggage. Juliette, who had always worn her lovely, thick black hair long, had just had it cut but had not yet begun to lose it, had not yet acquired what she called her "cancer look." A few days after our visit, Patrice shaved her head. From then on he did that once a week, carefully shaving her skull smooth. It was a moment of great intimacy and tenderness between them, he says. They'd wait until the girls weren't there, enjoying their time alone, making it last. I thought: Like a couple who meet to make love in the afternoon.

Unlike Étienne, who without being vulgar likes talking about sex so much that he feels no serious conversation should do without some, Patrice is rather prudish and I was surprised, looking through the panels of one of his comic strips full of willowy princesses and gallant knights, to spot an angel equipped with an obvious dick. When I ask him about it, he replies—unfazed— that during Juliette's pregnancy and after Diane's birth, desire had been at a low ebb between them, that to their joy it had quietly returned in the fall, but by then Juliette had grown more and more tired: there'd been her breathing problems, then the embolism, and so . . . they'd made love one more time, right after the news about the cancer. They'd both been clumsy, out of synch. He'd been afraid of hurting her. He hadn't known it would be the last time. Outside of intercourse, they had from the beginning had a very tender and close relationship, as if they'd been joined at the hip. They were always touching each other; they slept fitted together like two spoons. When one turned over, the other turned over as well; she would adjust her legs with her hands, and they'd wind up in the same position, facing the other direction: he'd fall asleep against her back and wake up with her against his, her knees folded into the hollow of his. This had become impossible with her illness. There was the oxygen tank, and she had to sleep with her upper body raised; the bedroom was like a hospital room. They had never been without their nightly intimacy until now and they missed it, but they still held hands and felt for each other in the dark, and even though the extent of their contact had diminished, Patrice does not remember a single night, up to the last, when their bodies weren't touching somewhere, at least a little bit.

At the end of February Juliette's condition was reviewed and found disappointing. There'd been no new metastases, the cancer was not progressing, but it wasn't regressing, either. That's what's so difficult with young patients, one doctor said; the cells prolif-erate so quickly . . . Honestly, they'd hoped for more from the treatment, which they decided to continue without any great con-viction, almost as if, thought Juliette, they just didn't know what else to do.

During the drive home, she told Patrice she'd avoided dealing with things long enough. It was time for her to get ready.

24

She made no secret of her illness. After her embolism, she'd told her neighbor Anne-Cécile: Listen, I had a real shock, I thought it was serious although now it seems it isn't, but it could have been, and you should know that I'm counting on you, for the girls. A month later, when the bad news hit, she shared it with their friends in her blunt, efficient way: I've got cancer, I'm not sure I'll make it, so I'm going to need you. Patrice and Juliette were very close to two other couples in the village, Philippe and Anne-Cécile, and Christine and Laurent. They had children the same age and matching lifestyles. They were all from elsewhere, not Rosier; in fact, few people in Rosier were from the village, and that's probably why newcomers fit in so easily. Their homes, where I had coffee occasionally, were furnished in the same cheery, unpretentious fashion, their mailboxes each decorated with a funny sticker drawn

by Patrice saying No Flyers Please. They had barbecues in their
yards, looked after one another's kids, and exchanged DVDs
(action films for the boys, romantic comedies for the girls), which
Patrice and Juliette watched on their computer because they were
the only villagers without a TV. This radical choice, a legacy from
Patrice's family, was the subject of constant teasing in their circle,
as was Patrice's tendency to take seriously even the most outland-
ish things anyone said. He and Philippe were like a vaudeville
team, the idealistic dreamer and the showy cynic, and Patrice
smilingly admitted that sometimes, when their wives formed an
affectionate audience, he might lay it on a bit thick as the inno-
cent dummy.

A few weeks before Juliette announced she had cancer, Anne-
Cécile had had some wonderful news: she was expecting. She
remembers as particularly horrible the parallel progress of her
pregnancy and her neighbor's illness. Both women suffered from
nausea, but Juliette's was from the chemo. One was carrying new
life, the other her own death. To welcome their fourth child, Anne-
Cécile and Philippe immediately began some major renovations in
their home, and Patrice and Juliette had talked about remodeling
as well: knocking down walls, repainting, transforming the basement into a real office. All four of them had been swept up in the
renovations, spreading floor plans, catalogs, color charts out on
tables, but now, for Patrice and Juliette, those plans had faded.
Anne-Cécile and Philippe were ashamed of being happy, of growing and prospering when misfortune had struck their friends, whose
lives had always been so like their own. Anne-Cécile felt that in
Juliette's place she couldn't have helped resenting her neighbors'
good fortune, and what often happens in such cases almost did:
awkwardness, uneasiness, visits falling off . . . But she came to understand that Juliette really didn't resent her contentment, that she took
a sincere interest in her pregnancy and her plans for the future.

Anne-Cécile and Philippe realized that they could keep sharing their happiness without feeling cruel or inappropriate and that they could be a help to their friends without having to look sad.

Late one March evening, on their way back from the Chinese restaurant in Vienne, Patrice and Juliette decided to drop by Anne-Cécile and Philippe's house. Juliette's parents were visiting for a few days, and they'd sent the couple off to dinner while they babysat the girls. The four friends went into the living room, where Philippe added fresh wood to the fire and suggested a whiskey, while Anne-Cécile offered to make herb tea. Juliette waited until they were all settled to tell them that her last checkup had been bad, that she and Patrice had discussed two important things over dinner, and she wanted to talk about them now. The first concerned her funeral. At these words, the other couple had the tact not to exclaim in well-intentioned protest, and I'm sure Juliette appreciated that. She said, Patrice is not religious, and I don't know about myself, it's complicated, but you two are. You're our only friends who are and I like the way you live your faith. I've thought about it and I'd like a Christian burial; it's less gloomy, people can come together, and anyway I just couldn't do other-wise, it would be awful for my parents. So I'd like you to be the ones to arrange that. All right? Fine, replied Anne-Cécile, as calmly as possible, and Philippe, always the joker, added solemnly, We'll plan the funeral as if it were our own.

Good, now the second thing. I know that if I die Diane won't consciously remember me. Amélie yes, Clara a little—but Diane no, and I'm really having trouble accepting this. Patrice takes pic-tures, of course, but Philippe, you're really good at it, and I'd like you to take as many pictures of me as you can from now on. If you take a whole bunch, maybe a few of them won't be too awful.

Philippe said he would and he did. But what was appalling, he remembers, was that the simple gesture of getting out his camera and pointing it at her began to mean: You are going to die.

Everything had to be wrapped up, the case files left in order, just as if she were going on vacation, and she was afraid she would run out of time. She didn't know how much time she had left, but she was pretty sure it wasn't much. She divided up tasks among her friends, asking everyone what they could do for her, and whatever was decided, that was it, she moved on. Philippe was in charge of the photos and the funeral mass. Anne-Cécile, a speech therapist, would be dealing with Clara's lisp, and Christine, a schoolteacher, would oversee the children's education. Laurent, a human resources manager, was promoted to chief financial officer, responsible for death benefits, home loan, social security for Patrice and the girls—all things that had been preying on Juliette's mind. She went over the choices with Laurent: long-term illness benefits or short-term death benefits? The long-term illness benefits entailed a reduction in salary, which was almost the more worrisome option, financially speaking, because the family budget was already tight. One solution was to cheat, to return to work for a week only to take another leave of absence; another solution was to opt for reduced work time in an environment adapted to her illness, but she wasn't sure she had the strength for that. When she died, the home loan would be paid off by insurance, and the administrator of the local justice ministry pension plan, whom Juliette and Laurent went to consult together, told them Patrice would be covered by her health plan for another two years. But after that?

* * *

Juliette was also preparing Patrice for life without her. At first he refused to have those conversations, finding them morbid, but once he realized they actually did them both some good, he began almost to look forward to them: they relieved the tension, and Juliette was calmer afterward. There was a kind of conjugal intimacy involved in sitting down at the table to talk about such things, a closeness that sometimes seemed completely unreal to him. In their marriage, she was the one who went off to work while he managed at home, so he didn't need instructions for domestic things, but she still wanted to go over everything, like a slightly obsessive landlord explaining to a new tenant where everything goes in the house, what days to take the garbage out, and when the boiler needs its annual maintenance inspection. The worst was the day she brought up the question of summer vacation, which she'd already figured out, with the girls staying for a few weeks with each of their two families. She thought it would be good for Patrice to have some time on his own, to rest, because the summer would be difficult for him. When he realized she meant the *coming* summer, Patrice felt dizzy for a moment, which she noticed. Taking his hand, she said she was saying this *just in case*, but neither of them was fooled.

When Patrice told me that, I thought about that summer, which had already passed. Hélène and I had taken Clara and Amélie for a week, as Juliette had planned, and we'd done our best to entertain them. Clara had clung to Hélène. In a bound notebook, in her lovely neat handwriting, Amélie had begun a novel in which the heroine was a princess, naturally, and I remember the opening line: Once upon a time there was a mother who had three daughters. And suddenly the images that were memories for me became Juliette's visions of a future yet to be: a few months earlier, Juliette had imagined those bike rides, those trips to the beach, those hugs and caresses steeped in grief, and she'd thought, I won't be there anymore. It will be my girls' first summer without me.

During the "internship" I spent at the *tribunal d'instance*, Mme Dupraz, the court clerk with whom Juliette had gotten along best, spoke to me about the guardianship of minors, which the two of them had dealt with every Tuesday. When one parent in a family dies leaving an inheritance to his or her children, the judge supervising a guardianship looks after the children's interests, monitoring the surviving parent's use of the capital. This must be explained to the remaining parent a month or two after the death of the spouse, and some don't appreciate what they see as an intrusion into their family life. The reality is that the widow or widower may not touch even a centime in the child's account without the judge's permission, and the banks are all the more strict on this provision because if they neglect it they may be responsible for reimbursing the account. Most requests to the judge are no problem, and Juliette soon became accustomed to signing whole stacks of payment orders in June, for the summer vacation, and December, for Christmas presents. There are cases, however, when the boundary between the child's interest and that of the parent is not clear. One can authorize the repair of a roof because the child is better off having a sound roof over his or her head. But isn't it also better for the child to have a father who isn't hounded by debt collectors? Does that mean the child's capital may serve to pay off paternal debts? This sort of thing depends on the judgment of the court, and great tact is required to make such arbitration as unintrusive as possible. Mme Dupraz told me that Juliette excelled in this very human form of justice, to which Patrice had just recently been introduced. Thinking about Patrice, Mme Dupraz remembered with some emotion the case of a young man who came before the tribunal. He had just lost his wife, had two little children, and the way he spoke about her and them, the simplicity and nobility of his grief, had deeply affected Juliette and Mme Dupraz. And he'd been handsome, too, so good-looking that it became a running joke with them to say, That guy, you know, we need to summon him more often. I wonder if Juliette, before she died, ever thought back to that episode, remembering that handsome, gentle widower so much at a loss. I wonder whether she imagined the interview Patrice would have in the office that had once been hers, and the impression he would make on the judge supervising his children's guardianship, two or three months after her death . . . Quite probably.

Philippe, who usually jogs early in the morning two or three times a week, persuaded Patrice to join him, to take his mind off his troubles for an hour or so. They ran on the country roads around Rosier, taking it easy, both because Patrice wasn't used to jogging and so that they could talk. Patrice confided in Philippe things he didn't dare say to Juliette. He reproached himself for not supporting her better, for even avoiding her at moments. It was hard for both of them to stay home all the time, Juliette collapsed on the sofa with her oxygen tank, trying to read, dozing, in pain, and not demanding that he be there, actually, while he hid in his basement workroom, vaguely pretending to be busy while he was really frantically playing video games. Martin, the thirteen-year-old son of Laurent and Christine, sometimes joined him down there, where they spent hours flying planes or mowing down enemy hordes with bazookas. Juliette didn't like him to waste time like that but understood that he sometimes needed to anesthetize himself. As soon as he stopped, the merry-go-round in his head would start up again: fear, pity, shame, infinite love, and questions without answers. No longer *Will she die?* but *When will she die?* Could they have done anything to save her? If they'd found the tumor earlier, would that have made a difference? Did the first cancer have anything to do with Chernobyl, and the second with the high-tension line fifty yards from the house they used to live in? He'd read a truly alarming study about power lines in an antinuclear magazine to which he subscribed. This kind of pointless nonsense, as they put it, drove Juliette's parents crazy. Patrice had learned to keep quiet on that score but he still thought about such things, and they ate away at him.

Listening to him, Philippe became worried, fearing Patrice would break down after Juliette's death. Philippe himself admits that he might do the same after a shock like that: if Anne-Cécile died, his world would collapse, leaving him not just miserable but lost, unable to cope. And today Philippe is all the more impressed to see that Patrice didn't break down, he weathered the shock and is coping. When others remark on this, Patrice replies, I take life as it comes. I have three daughters to raise, and that's what I'm doing. He hardly ever seems depressed. He's bearing up. Good for him, says Philippe.

As for Juliette, outside of the tasks she assigned to her friends, she hardly ever confided in them, if by that one means saying things it's useless to say and about which the other person can't do anything. Juliette would have called that complaining, and she didn't want to complain. When Anne-Cécile or Christine dropped by in the afternoon for a chat and a cup of tea, she'd say the days were passing slowly, between the sofa and the armchair, in a constant state of drowsy nausea, and that she didn't have the strength to read, could barely watch a film, that life was shrinking and it wasn't funny, but more than that she would not say. What was the point?

She was suffering, and said so, from not being able to take more care of her girls. How could she go see Amélie dance in the theater in Vienne when she was so exhausted she couldn't even read them bedtime stories anymore? Just when she should have been taking advantage of what were doubtless the last moments of their life together, she wanted only one thing every evening: for Patrice to put them to bed so that she could go to sleep. She could have just wept. And then Juliette, who never repeated her instructions, would return again to her overwhelming concern: You'll talk to them about me, right? You'll tell them I tried hard? That I did everything I could not to leave them?

She worried about her parents, too. If it had been up to them, they'd have moved to Rosier to hover over her, to at least be near her in the dreadful helplessness to which they had been reduced, but after they'd been there a few days Juliette wanted them to go. They'd tried hard, but the way they looked at Patrice wounded her, his uneasiness humiliated her, and besides, they didn't belong there. Their presence would have turned her back into the little girl she did not wish to be again, the one they'd protected from her first cancer seventeen years before. When Juliette said "my family," she meant the one she'd made with Patrice, not the one into which she was born. Time and energy were running out; she wanted to devote the little she had left to the life she had chosen, not the one she'd inherited. And yet she loved her parents. She knew how much it hurt them to be kept at a distance from her death and wished she could help them face it, but she didn't know how to comfort them. Neither Christine nor Anne-Cécile could do anything for her there.

Her girlfriends would willingly have had a heart-to-heart, as they put it, but whenever they made any veiled reference to her presumed anguish over her illness, she fended them off, saying, No, I'm okay. For that stuff I have Étienne.

* * *

One day I said to Étienne, I didn't know Juliette, I have no place mourning her, nothing authorizes me to write about this. His reply was, That's what *gives* you the authority, and in a way it's the same for me. Her illness wasn't my illness. When she told me about her cancer, I thought, Phew! It's her and not me, and perhaps because I thought that, and because I wasn't ashamed of thinking that, I was able to do her a little good. At one point, to be more *present* to her, I tried to remember my second cancer, my fear of death, the frightening loneliness—and it didn't work. I could remember it, of course, but not feel it. I thought, so much the better. She's the one who's going to die, not me. Her death devastated me as few things have in my life, but it did not invade me. I was facing her, near her, but in my place.

She was always the one who phoned, not him. He never said anything comforting to her but she, she could say everything, without fear of hurting him. Everything, meaning the horror. The moral horror of imagining the world without her, of knowing she would never see her girls grow up, but also the physical horror, which was increasing. The horror of a body in revolt because it senses the approach of annihilation. The horror of learning at each checkup that the situation has changed, always for the worse: you try to think there can't be only bad news, but, yes, there can. The horror of treatments, of endless futile pain, with no hope of getting better, only of taking longer to die. In April she told Étienne, I can't go on; it's too hard, I'm stopping. You have the right, he told her. You've done all you can, no one can ask you to keep going. Stop, if you want.

Étienne's permission helped her. She kept it in reserve, like a cyanide capsule in case of torture, and she decided to keep going a little further. She'd expected to be relieved the day the doctors told her, Listen, there's nothing else we can do, we're going to let you alone now, so she was surprised to feel so stricken when that day came, in May. They told her they were stopping the Herceptin, which was giving her heart problems without the slightest benefit in return. They didn't deliver the news as bluntly as she'd anticipated, but it boiled down to them giving up, and Juliette, who was no longer thinking in terms of years of reprieve but of months, now understood it was a question of weeks, perhaps of days.

25

—

Right after the Herceptin was stopped in May 2005, Patrice and Juliette had a violent argument over the referendum on the European Constitution. Patrice was so strongly against approval that he abandoned his video games to post messages on Web forums. It was his new drug. He'd come upstairs from the basement with marked-up printouts of documents he'd found on Attac, a site opposed to the constitution. One could and should, he argued, resist the absolute rule of free market ideology, which it was immoral to consider as inevitable. Juliette let him talk on without expressing her opinion, and that reminded him of her silence at the outbreak of the first Gulf War, when they had just met. He'd been against intervention, denouncing the manipulations of the media, and since she'd kept quiet, he'd thought she agreed with him until, forced to take a stand, she'd admitted she didn't. Without being really in favor of the war, she wasn't as against it as he was—not as sure, in any case, of what she thought. He was stunned. Why hadn't she said so? Why hadn't she *argued*? Because she knew he would never change his mind and she saw no point in shouting at each other for nothing, that's all. But this time, they did end up shouting, each one attacking the other's family and Patrice, not without reason, tossing in Étienne for good measure. Once Juliette even told Patrice that after her death she hoped he would meet a cute alter-globalist who'd be hipper and nicer than a cancer-riddled right-leaning bitch of a wife. In the end, she had him cast her "yes" vote by proxy, which he did the week before she died.

What led Patrice to tell me about that last quarrel, with more tenderness than regret, was my asking him if he imagined himself having a love life again one day. The question didn't shock him but left him thoughtful. Perhaps Juliette was right; perhaps he'd remake his life with a hip, nice alter-globalist, why not? That's what he deserved. But one of the things he'd loved in Juliette was that she wasn't the woman with whom he would ordinarily have wound up. She had jolted him out of his rut. She was different, the unexpected, the miracle that arrives just once in a lifetime—and only if you're lucky. That's why I don't complain, concluded Patrice. I was lucky.

On Wednesday, June 8, he brought home a video of a film by Agnès Jaoui, *Comme une image* (*Look at Me*). After the girls were asleep, he and Juliette sat on the living room sofa watching the movie on a computer set up in front of them on a footstool. Juliette was wearing her oxygen mask but didn't feel too bad. She fell asleep before the end, on his shoulder, the way she almost always did those days when they watched a film or he read to her. He stayed there without moving, afraid to wake her. He sat listening to her breathe and had the feeling, simply by being there, that he was protecting her. In return for these peaceful moments, he would have been ready to have this life of theirs—however terrible—go on for a long time. Forever, even. With infinite care, he carried her to their room and put her to bed. Then he fell asleep, holding her hand. At four in the morning, she suddenly began to cough uncontrollably. She couldn't breathe: the oxygen at top flow brought no relief; it was as if she were drowning. As in December, he called an ambulance, then Christine, so she could stay with the girls. Christine wanted to come into the bedroom while they waited for the ambulance but Juliette, through the door, said, No, no, and today Christine is sorry she didn't move out of the hall when Juliette was carried past her to the ambulance. She feels she didn't respect the wishes of her friend, who hadn't wanted to be seen in such a state. But she told Patrice she'd take care of everything, that he could stay all day and even the next night at the hospital, which he did. In the intensive care unit, Juliette's blood oxygen level returned to normal, yet she continued to struggle for breath. She was given morphine, which brought her some relief. Two liters of liquid were drained from the pleura around her right lung, but in vain. That was on Thursday. On Friday morning, the chief of oncology came to tell her that they could do no more for her, that her body had reached the end of its defenses and she would die within days, perhaps within hours. Juliette replied that she was ready. She asked for her parents, brother, and sisters to be called; if they arrived that afternoon or evening, she would be able to say good-bye to them. As for her daughters, Juliette did not want to spoil the older girls' participation in their school festival, and she asked the doctor if he could make sure she'd be able to see them in twenty-four hours. He told her that yes, they would administer the morphine in such a way that she would be neither in too much pain nor too knocked out by sedation. Then Juliette had the entire medical team that had treated her since February come to her room, where she thanked each person, one by one. She was not upset with them because the treatments had failed; she was sure they had done everything in their power, as humanely as they could. After that, she sent Patrice home to take care of the girls and talk to them. While he was gone, she would see Étienne.

Étienne: I was ahead of her in my legal career, and also where cancer was concerned. We were on the same path, and it was clear to both of us that I had gone before her. But that Friday afternoon, she went on ahead of me. She told me, Étienne, you are one of the few people who have given meaning to my life and thanks to whom I have really lived it. I think that despite my illness, it's been a good life. I look at my life, and I'm content with it. And I, continues Étienne, I who never stop talking, I didn't know what to say. She had come to a place where I could no longer follow her. So I said—The letter, have you written it? That was something we'd talked a great deal about, that letter she wanted to leave to her girls. She'd started lots of drafts but thrown them out each time because she was overwhelmed, there was too much to say, or almost nothing: I love you, I loved you, be happy. No, she told me sadly, I haven't written it, so I said we should do it. Right now? Yes, now, why not? Let's start with—what would you say to your girls about Patrice? She was having more and more trouble speaking, but she answered immediately: He was my all. He carried me. She paused, then added, He's the father I chose for you. You, too: *choose* in life. You can ask everything of him; he will give you everything you ask for while you're little, and when you're grown up, *you* will choose. She thought a moment, then said, That's it.

I took no notes; when I got home I wrote the letter in two minutes: it was done. I gave it to her sister Cécile, who read it to her and told me Juliette had nodded to show it was good. But before I left her room that afternoon, I sat on the edge of her bed and held her hand for a few moments. I'd shaken her hand when she'd first entered my office six years before, but after that, and until that Friday afternoon, we'd never touched again.

Patrice found his mother at home with the girls; she'd just arrived to take over from Christine. The children weren't too frightened; Juliette's hospital stays were now part of ordinary life for them. What they did want to know was whether she would be at the school show, and when their father said no, they protested: She'd promised! Then Patrice told them she would not be coming home, that they'd all go to the hospital after the school festival the next day, and it would be for the last time, because she was going to die. He held Diane in his arms and spoke to her as much as to her older sisters, even though she was only fifteen months old. He remembers that Amélie and Clara cried and screamed, that this went on for an hour, and then they were out of control until bedtime, completely overexcited. Strangely enough, everyone managed to sleep. Patrice returned to the hospital quite early the next morning, so that he could then be on time for the beginning of the school show. Juliette's condition had deteriorated further during the night. She was quite agitated, and her eyes kept rolling back into her head. All her remaining strength was now devoted to breathing harshly, painfully, in spasms that shook her whole body. Sensing his presence, she clung to Patrice's arm and exclaimed several times in a bitter voice, rocking back and forth, So, it's over now! So, it's over now! Patrice tried to talk to her, very gently, to tell her that the girls would come to see her after the school festival, but Juliette didn't seem to understand and kept saying, So, it's over now! Patrice was appalled, both because the girls might see her like this and because when Juliette had told him she was no longer afraid of dying, he'd believed her. What was unbearable, she had said, was leaving her little family, but death, she'd prepared herself, it would be all right. Such stoicism was her way, she would have wanted to leave that image of herself, but what Patrice saw now was a body wracked with suffering, prey to something like panic. Her clear mind, serenity . . . gone. She was losing control. This wasn't Juliette anymore. He went to see the nurses, who told him it was the effect of Atarax, an antihistamine with sedative and antinausea properties, and they assured him that, as promised, they'd do their best to have her as calm and lucid as possible for her daughters' visit. All their efforts worked only halfway, however, and when Patrice and Cécile led in the girls, Juliette was barely conscious. If you spoke to her from close up, her gaze would fix on you for a second before wandering off. Her head bobbed once or twice, which could have been taken for acquiescence. Amélie and Clara had made drawings for her and they'd brought a video of the school show, but in spite of its importance to the girls—and to Juliette herself only the day before—Patrice didn't have the heart to play the video on the TV in the room. The situation was so painful that the visit was cut short. Clara kissed her mother, Patrice held Diane's face against her cheek, but Amélie was so frightened that she wouldn't leave her aunt's arms.

At this point in Patrice's story, a barefoot Amélie came into the living room in her pajamas. She'd been put to bed long before but must have awakened and heard our discussion through her half-open bedroom door. This didn't bother Patrice, who'd started talking to me about Juliette's last days while his daughters were present and without lowering his voice. Amélie planted herself in front of us and said, It's even harder for me than for Diane and Clara that Mama died because I didn't say good-bye to her, I was scared. Patrice assured her calmly that she hadn't kissed her but she had said good-bye, that the important thing was that she was there, and her mama had seen her. I gathered from his tone that this wasn't the first time they'd talked about this, and while he put Amélie back to bed, I thought it was a good thing that she was able to voice her self-reproach: once expressed, that guilt was less likely to poison her life later on without her even recognizing why. And since I have good reason to think that the psychoanalytic faith in the healthy powers of speech (as opposed to the ravages of silence) is well founded, I commended Patrice sincerely when he returned, for letting his entire attitude show his girls that things should be *said*.

The visits over, Patrice remained alone with Juliette. She was less agitated, but the serenity he'd hoped for was not there. Sitting next to her on the bed, he tried to communicate with her, to sense her desires. When he helped her drink, she managed to swallow. Her chest began to heave spasmodically; as her body grew tense he felt her hour had come, but no, she wasn't dying, she was suffering. Drawn toward the void, she was fighting back. He asked her, Are you afraid? She nodded, emphatically. Wait, he said, I'll help you. I'm coming back. Don't worry, I'm coming back. He pried himself away from her as gently as he could and found her doctor to tell him that she needed his help, now. Right, the doctor replied, wait for me here. And when Hélène and I went to the same office a half hour later to ask the same thing of the same doctor, he told us they had begun to take care of it.

The five minutes he spent alone in the office were an eternity for Patrice. He stared numbly at the chipped paint on a base-board, the neon tube on the ceiling, the gnat flitting around the tube, the summer night beginning to fall outside, framed in the window, and he felt that all the world's reality was there, nothing else existed, had ever existed, would ever exist. When he went back into Juliette's room, her eyes—half closed when he'd left her—were shut. Some time later, he became terrified that she'd slipped into a coma during his brief absence. That she had seen a stranger come into her room and do something (it didn't matter what—a shot or an adjustment to the intravenous drip) and had believed, in her semiconscious state, that the intruder had come to finish her off. Patrice feared that her last thought before every-thing went dark had been: I'm dying, and Patrice isn't here. In the days that followed, he was so tormented by this horror scenario—which did not occur to him at the time, fortunately—that he finally called the doctor, who reassured him. Things couldn't have happened that way: that dosage of morphine takes more than an hour to act, and Juliette's slide into unconsciousness had been very gradual.

Patrice stretched out beside her again, but this time more com-fortably, almost as if they were home in bed. She was breathing calmly, seemingly without pain, drifting in a twilight state that at some point would become death, and he stayed with her until that moment. He began talking to her, very softly, and as he spoke he gently touched her hands, her face, her chest, and now and then he kissed her, lightly. Although convinced her brain could no longer analyze the vibrations of his voice or the touch of his skin, he was sure that her flesh could still sense them, that she was entering the unknown enveloped by something loving and familiar. He was there. He told her about their life and the happiness she'd given him. He told her how he had loved to laugh with her, to talk about anything and everything with her, and even to argue with her. He promised he would continue without fail to take good care of the girls, she mustn't worry. He would remember to put on their scarves, they wouldn't catch cold. He sang the songs she loved, described the instant of death as a great flash, an unbelievable wave of peace, a blessed return to the fount of all energy. One day he, too, would experience that and would rejoin her. Those words came easily to him; he spun them out in a low, calm voice, and they mesmerized him, too. It was life that hurt, by resisting, but the torment of being alive was ending. The nurse had told him that it was the patients who struggled who died the quickest. If Juliette was taking so long, Patrice thought, it might be because she had stopped fighting, that what still lived in her was tranquil, at rest. Don't fight it anymore, my love, let go, let go, let yourself go.

Toward midnight, though, he thought it wasn't possible, just wasn't possible that she could still be in that state another day. He decided that if at four in the morning she was still this way, he would unplug the breathing apparatus. At one, though, he couldn't stand the waiting anymore, thought Juliette might be communicating her own impatience to him, and went to find the nurse on duty to ask if someone could unplug the machine, because he felt it was time. She said no, that might be too brutal, it was better to let things take their course. Later, he fell asleep. A helicopter woke him shortly before three, hovering for a long time over the hospital. Patrice now kept his eyes glued to the clock. At a quarter to four Juliette's breathing, which had become a mere wisp of air, ceased. He watched for another few moments but there was nothing more: her heart had stopped beating. He told himself that she'd guessed what he meant to do at four and had spared him that pain.

* * *

Patrice keeps talking, telling his story, as if he never wants it to end.

I didn't need to close her eyes. I gazed at her: her face was lovely and serene, not like in those final days. I thought, She is my wife, and she is dead. My wife is dead. I felt her warmth ebb away and was astonished at how quickly that happened. By four o'clock, she was cold. I got up, I informed the nurses, I called Cécile, who was awake back at the house, and then I went outside, to walk around the hospital grounds. I could see a strip of sky growing light in the east, and pink clouds over the city; it was magnificent. I was relieved that everything was over but above all, at that moment, I felt immense affection for Juliette. I don't know how to put this; affection seems like a feeble word, but I felt something greater and stronger than love. A few hours later, at the hospital funeral parlor, the feeling had already changed. Love, yes, but that vast affection, it was gone.

26

Before leaving Juliette that Friday, Étienne had asked her if she would like him to come back or simply to remain available, and she'd said, To be available. He spent the night in waiting, suspecting she would not call again. They had said everything to each other; now there was no place left for anyone but Patrice. In the morning, he took the bus to the hospital but got off two stops early and went home. He spent Saturday with his family, ran some errands at a sporting goods store with his kids, tried to work. Juliette had asked that he be informed as soon as she died; it was Patrice's mother who called him at five the next morning, which made him angry, he remembers, because she woke him up and especially because she said, "Juliette has passed away" instead of "Juliette is dead." He growled, I know, I know, and when she invited him to view the body at the hospital funeral home he replied no, he wasn't interested.

Étienne and I had lunch together in Vienne the day after my long nocturnal conversation with Patrice, and Étienne accompanied me back to Rosier. The first thing he said when he got there was that he had to leave right away. Patrice and he had not seen each other since the funeral, and they seemed to feel a little awkward together, but I offered to make coffee so we could have it outside, under the catalpa, where we wound up spending the afternoon, more and more content to be with one another.

I remember two moments of that afternoon.

Patrice talked about how he and the girls were learning to live without Juliette. She carries me along, he said; her energy lifts me up . . . and then sometimes it doesn't carry me anymore. The nights are tough. At first I thought I'd never manage to sleep without her. My body was so used to hers that I think I feel her against me, and then I wake up, she's not there, and I'm lost, utterly lost. But I'm gradually getting used to it; I know that with time her presence will fade. I know some day fifteen minutes will go by without my thinking of her, and then an hour . . . I try to explain this to the girls . . . When I tell them we were lucky to be with her and love her and have her love us, Clara says that Amélie is the luckiest because she had her the longest, and Diane's lucky because she doesn't really understand, so she, being in the middle, has the hardest time . . . In spite of everything, I think we're in a good place, the four of us. I think it'll work. And you?

Patrice had turned to Étienne, who was startled by his question. Me, what?

You, insisted Patrice. How is it for you, life without Juliette?

Later, Étienne told me he'd been stunned, then deeply moved
to have been thus included in the circle of mourning—and by the
widower—almost on an equal footing. In his heart of hearts, he
found that position justified (Étienne's note: "Not entirely; I felt
justified simply in being included"), but he never would have
claimed it on his own. It took Patrice's incredible generosity to
acknowledge his place.

But out in the garden that day, Étienne gave a little laugh.
"For me? Oh, that's simple. What I miss is being able to talk to
her. It's quite selfish; as usual I'm thinking only of myself in this,
and what I find is that until I die there will be things I can no
longer tell a soul. It's over. The one person to whom I could have
said them without its being sad is gone."

Later, we talked about the slide show Patrice was putting
together for the family and friends in memory of Juliette. He'd
made a first, large selection of photos, and now he was winnow-
ing them down. Certain pictures virtually picked themselves; he
lingered long over others, and when he discarded any he did so
with a pang and the impression, each time, of condemning to
oblivion a moment of their life together. He was working on this
project at night in his basement workshop, after putting the girls
to bed. It was a moment he loved, both sad and sweet. He wasn't
rushing to finish his slide show, knowing that when he'd finally
sent everyone a copy of the finished product a milestone would
have been passed, one that he wasn't all that eager to reach, at
least not right away.

A bit like the letter Juliette wanted to write to the girls, remarked
Étienne. She kept promising herself to do it and putting it off
because she knew once she'd finished it she'd have nothing left
to do.

We fell silent. Across the village square, there was an explo-
sion of shouting and laughter as school let out. Amélie and Clara

would be home in a few minutes, expecting their afternoon snack, and soon Diane would need to be picked up. It was then Étienne said, There's one photo that won't be in your slide show because it doesn't exist, but if it did and I could keep only one, I'd choose it, no question. One evening, you remember, the four of us went to the theater in Lyon. Juliette and you, Nathalie and I. We arrived first and were waiting for you in the lobby. We saw you enter downstairs, and you carried her up the grand staircase. She had her arms around your neck, she was smiling, and what was beautiful was that she looked not only happy but proud, incredibly proud, and so did you. Everyone watched you two and stepped aside to let you pass. It really was the knight carrying the princess.

Patrice was silent for a moment, then smiled, with that astonished and dreamy smile with which you recognize a truth you've never thought of before. It's funny, now that you mention it, he said, I've always liked that, carrying people . . . Even as a kid, I carried my younger brother. I'd put the little kids in a wheelbarrow and push them, or I'd hoist them up on my shoulders . . .

On the train back to Paris, I wondered if there was a formula as simple and right as that—he liked to carry, she had to be carried—to define what bound us together, Hélène and I. I didn't find one, but thought that one day, perhaps, we would.

27

—

When I got back from Rosier, Hélène's breasts had begun to swell and she announced that she was pregnant. I should have been overjoyed but instead I felt afraid. The only explanation I can find for my fear is that I didn't feel ready: too many tethers were still in place, too many knots hadn't been sliced through. To be a father again in the second half of my life, I would have had to be a son fairly at peace with himself, and I thought myself far from that. I give myself this: despite my dismay, I decided it was better to say yes than no, and more or less consciously, feeling my way, I endeavored to change. My project had become inopportune, so I called Patrice and Étienne to let them know I was abandoning it, adding that I might perhaps return to it one day, although I doubted it. Étienne said, See what happens. I began to write directly about myself, the disaster of my previous love affair, and the ghost haunting my family, a ghost I wished to lay to rest. The gestation of that book lasted as long as Hélène's pregnancy, and it's an understatement to say those months were difficult, but I finished the job shortly after Jeanne's birth, and overnight the miracle for which I'd hoped without believing in it took place: the fox gnawing at my vitals went away. I was free. I spent a year enjoying the simple fact of being alive and watching our daughter grow. I had no ideas about what would come next, but no worries, either. Freud's definition of mental health has always appealed to me, even though it seemed beyond reach: the ability to love and work. I was able to love and, even better, to accept being loved; work would come in its own time. Somewhat at random, without knowing where I was going, I began to gather my memories of Sri Lanka, then took another look at my notes on Étienne, Patrice, Juliette, and consumer law. I returned to this book three years after conceiving the project; I've finished it three years after abandoning the whole thing.

This time, I resolved to let those my book concerned read it before publication. I'd already done that with Jean-Claude Romand, but I'd warned him that *The Adversary* was finished and I would not change a single line. Submitting *My Life as a Russian Novel*, the memoir I wrote while Hélène was pregnant, for the approval of my mother and Sophie, my ex, would have been like heaving it into a bonfire, a luxury I could not afford, so I presented them with the fait accompli. I don't regret that, it saved my life, but I wouldn't do it again. Hélène was the first to read these pages. She had accepted my undertaking this project, but the closer I came to the end, the more she dreaded discovering what I'd written about Juliette. She still cannot believe in her death or talk about her; perhaps she reproaches herself for not having truly understood her sister. Once she'd read the book, we were both relieved, and I sent the text to Étienne and Patrice, telling them that they could ask me to add, remove, or change whatever they wanted, and I would. This promise worried Paul, my publisher, who reminded me that people are never happy with how they appear in books, and once my main characters had set their records straight, my book would be a shambles. As it happened, he was wrong, and in the end my last trip to Lyon and Rosier was for me and for Patrice and Étienne as well, I believe, the most moving visit of this entire endeavor. I felt like a portrait painter who, on displaying his canvas, hopes that the model will be pleased, and both of them were. Étienne told me, There are some things I completely disagree with, but I'll be very careful not to tell you which, for fear you might change them. I like that this is *your* book, and on the whole I also like the guy in it who's got my name. I can even tell you this: I'm rather proud. Although Étienne didn't have me cut anything, he did ask me to add a few items, to give credit where credit was due. When I told the story of the appeal to the ECJ, I had focused, for the sake of dramatic economy, on the Juliette-Étienne-Florès troika, without mentioning Bernadette Le Baut-Ferrarese, the EU law specialist who advised them, and Étienne found it unfair to leave her out of the picture. As for Patrice, he was afraid I had overemphasized the political disagreements he'd had with Juliette. He kept coming back to that, quibbling, correcting, clarifying nuances. It didn't bother him to pass for a naïve leftist, but he refused to let anyone believe Juliette had the slightest leaning to the right, and I felt to my amazement that I was hearing him pursue, through my book, the trusting and passionate discussion he and Juliette had carried on throughout their thirteen years together. After our work on the text, when we went to fetch the girls at school, several of Amélie's classmates surrounded me and asked, Is it true you wrote a book about Juliette? Can we read it? But when I broached the subject at dinner with Amélie herself and her two sisters, they hardly reacted at all. Yes, we know, they said and, looking away, they changed the subject.

We'd gone to see Philippe, Delphine, and Jérôme in Saint-Émilion a few months after our return from Sri Lanka. Little Juliette's room was a shrine; it was horribly sad. Then Philippe wrote his book, and we exchanged a few affectionate yet distant e-mails. Camille was born a year later, ten days after Jeanne, and there again we exchanged birth announcements and left it at that. So it was after two years of silence that I contacted Philippe once more, sending him the manuscript, asking him both to read it and to help ease his daughter and son-in-law into taking a look. Aside from one topographic detail, Philippe found everything fine but thought it better that Delphine and Jérôme not read the text. Not then, at any rate, and perhaps not ever. Later on, the four of us— Hélène, Rodrigue, Jeanne, and I—spent a weekend with them and had a delightful time. They'd just had another child, a boy, Antoine, not even a month old. The two little girls got along immediately. Rodrigue, who adores Delphine, was happy to see her again, and she him. I passed along news of Jean-Baptiste, who was studying at an Irish university, and of his older brother, Gabriel, a fledgling film editor. Philippe told us how his aid association for the fishermen of Medaketiya had sprung up, then closed down after accomplishing its mission. He still goes back there for three or four months every year. From his beach bungalow, he looks at the ocean. He thinks about his life; sometimes he manages not to think about anything. The evening passed the way evenings do chez Delphine and Jérôme: commenting on the wines in a blind tasting, listening to rare Rolling Stones records, smoking

home-grown pot, and laughing, laughing a lot. Juliette's room is
no longer a shrine, it's Camille's bedroom and she'll share it with
Antoine when he's a little bigger, but there is a photo of Juliette
on the mantelpiece and no one has any trouble saying her name.
Delphine and Jérôme have not two children but three, it's just
that one of them is dead.

When we got around to talking about my book, Delphine said
she did mean to read it, but Philippe, with that suddenly shrill,
quavering voice he'd had over there, warned her off: it would be
particularly difficult for her because she would learn things that
had been hidden from her. Puzzled, I asked him later in private
what he'd meant. He'd been thinking of the moment when
Jérôme, returning from the morgue in Colombo, tells Delphine
that Juliette is still beautiful, then admits to Hélène that he was
lying: their little girl is decomposing. Can you imagine, said
Philippe, Delphine discovering in your book that Jérôme lied to
her? I offered to remove that detail if he thought it more painful
than the others, but he said there was no question of that, and by
the time we'd finished our talk, he allowed as how Delphine
would see her husband's lie not as a betrayal but as one more
proof of his love. It was decided in the end that Philippe would
pass the book on to Jérôme, who would then give it to Delphine,
if he thought that appropriate. I recognized in that order of precedence the way her two men, her father and her husband, had
banded together to protect her over there, but when I said this to
Hélène, she shook her head and said, She's the one protecting
them, you know—she's the one who holds everything together.
That they remained a couple, had other children, that life won
out in the end, it's thanks to her. Then I remembered something
Delphine had just said during dinner: the moment over there
when life carried the day, when she chose to live instead of letting
herself go under, was when she agreed to watch Rodrigue while

we were gone. At first she'd thought, No, take care of a child two days after my daughter died, I just couldn't, but she'd said yes, and from then on she'd continued, despite everything, to say yes.

This morning, Jeanne woke up at seven, climbed out of her crib the way she has learned to do, and joined us in our bed. I went to the kitchen to prepare her bottle, which she drank lying between us without too much noise or squirming, but that respite never lasts long, for soon there must be songs and games. Her favorite song at the moment is "Mister Bear." Snoring mightily with my back turned and the duvet pulled over my head, I play the Bear. Hélène sings: Mister Bear, wake up, you've slept quite enough, when I count three, time to get up! One. Two. Three! Mister Bear? Can you hear me? And the first time, in my deepest voice, I answer: Nope. Hélène tries again: Mister Bear! Can you hear me? This time I turn over, growling, Yup! Hélène and Jeanne imitate the children's squeals of fear on the song tape, and Jeanne is in heaven. Mister Bear will last only one season; before him there were the Three Little Kittens who'd lost their mittens, and when Jeanne happens to open the musical book of the Three Little Kittens with its failing batteries, Hélène and I already feel something akin to nostalgia: that's the song from when she was tiny, barely toddling and not yet talking, and that miraculous time is already past, never to return. I think about all those childish things that enchant us and about what torture they must become if the unspeakable happens: the nursery rhymes, toys, fuzzy slippers all survive while the little girl is rotting in a box underground. And yet that enchantment became possible again for Delphine and Jérôme, with their two other children. They haven't forgotten anything, but they did not stay lost in the abyss. I find that admirable, incomprehensible, mysterious. That's the best word: mysterious.

Later, I fix our breakfast while Hélène dresses Jeanne. When
I say that she dresses her, it's not simply that she puts her clothes
on; she chooses them and buys them with perhaps even more
pleasure and feminine chic than when she shops for herself, which
means that Jeanne is the best-dressed little girl in the world. They
join me in the kitchen. Hélène wears yoga pants and a light pull-
over with a low neckline; the pants cling to her buttocks and the
top shows the outline of her nipples. She's lovely, sexy, tender. I'm
dazzled by the tranquillity of our love and by the intensity of this
tranquillity. At her side, I know where I am. I can't bear the idea
of losing her, but for the first time in my life I believe that what
might steal her from me, or me from her, would be an accident,
illness, something that would strike us from outside—and not
dissatisfaction, ennui, a craving for something new. It's rash to say
that, but really, I don't think that would happen. I suspect, of
course, that if we last long enough there will be crises, empty
stretches, stormy patches; desire will flag and go looking elsewhere,
but I believe we'll hold together, that one of us will close the other's
eyes. In any case, that's what I long for.

   In the front hall, Jeanne and I put on our coats and she takes
a firm grip on her stroller—not the one her parents push her
around in (and in which she sits with less and less good grace
these days) but the miniature one she uses for a rather ratty-
looking bald doll made of plastic that smells like strawberry
chewing gum. Ever since Hélène bought her that stroller, Jeanne
insists on taking it with her when she goes out. In general, she
wants to do everything we do, and since we take our child out for
walks, she wants to do the same. So we roll the stroller out onto
the landing, and Hélène crouches in the front doorway of the
apartment to give her daughter one last kiss. Jeanne starts to get
into the elevator as I hold the door open, but she pauses, turns
around to wave bye to Hélène, and only then steps in and reaches

up on tiptoe to push the right button. Just before the glass-fronted door sinks below the landing, I see Hélène smile at us. We step outside, Jeanne pushing her stroller and me walking beside her, making sure she doesn't wind up in the street. She's so proud of imitating us that she forgets to dawdle and stop at each doorway, each lamppost, each scooter the way she usually does. She's being responsible, heading straight down the sidewalk of the rue d'Hauteville almost as fast as if I'd been pushing her. She looks back occasionally so that I notice she's doing everything correctly. When we reach her nanny's building, I hoist Jeanne up to the keypad and, as I do every morning, guide her fingers over it. Next in our ritual come the timer switch for the staircase light, the doorbell, and listening at Mme Laouni's door for her footsteps coming down the hall. Jeanne never protests when I take her to Mme Laouni's place. She's comfortable there; Mme Laouni is both affectionate and firm, so one feels she runs a tight, happy ship. Last year, though, she lost her husband. She phoned one morning in tears to tell us she couldn't watch Jeanne because her husband had died during the night: she'd found him dead of a heart attack next to her in bed. Before that, she'd seemed like a happy woman, at home in life. Never any bitterness, lassitude, sloppiness. Order, good humor, dynamism, kindness. And that impression hasn't changed since her husband's death. I know nothing about their life as a couple; I'd never met him, since he left for work before I brought Jeanne and returned after I'd picked her up, but I'm sure Mme Laouni loved him, that they were good partners, fine parents for their daughters, that she misses him dreadfully, that life without him is sad, unfair, unnatural, and what impresses me is that her grief, which she doesn't hide when we speak with her, never seems to weigh on the children she cares for. She says they are the ones who help her keep going, and I believe her. Sometimes, when she opens her door in the morning,

I can see that her eyes are puffy, that she must have been crying in the night, that it was hard for her to get up, but when she takes Jeanne in her arms the child laughs, Mme Laoumi laughs with her, and I know it will be like that all day long.

I go back up the rue d'Hauteville. I will be stopping at the café on the place Franz-Liszt to read the paper and then going home. Rodrigue will have left for school, Hélène has perhaps gone back to bed, in which case I'll join her and we'll make love in that peaceful, slightly routine conjugal way that inspires in both of us an ever-renewed and I trust inexhaustible desire. I'll make fresh coffee that we'll drink in the kitchen while talking about the children, friends, domestic details, and what's going on in the world. She'll leave for work, and it will be time for me to get to mine, too. Every day for six months I deliberately spent several hours at the computer writing about what frightens me the most on this earth: the death of a child for her parents and the death of a young woman for her husband and children. Life made me a witness to those two misfortunes, one right after the other, and assigned me—at least that's how I understood it—to tell that story. Life has spared me such unhappiness and I pray will continue to do so. I've sometimes heard it said that happiness is best understood in retrospect. One thinks: I didn't realize it at the time, but I was happy. That doesn't work for me. I was miserable for a long time and quite conscious of it. I love my lot in life now (no great achievement, since it's so pleasant), and my philosophy can be summed up in the remark made on the evening of her son's coronation by Madame Letizia, the mother of Napoleon, who murmured, "Let's hope it lasts."

And one more thing: I prefer what I have in common with other people to what sets me apart from them. That, too, is new.

Having reached the end of this book, I find something is missing. It concerns Diane. Amélie and Clara have small speaking roles, and each has a scene to herself like her very own bedroom, but when everything happened Diane was so little that she appears only as a quiet or squalling baby in her father's arms. She's four now, and I think she tells herself what her sisters thought, each for her own reason: that it's even harder for her. Because she's the last child, because she had her mother for only fifteen months, because she doesn't even remember her. Nathalie, Étienne's wife, told me that the last time they visited the family in Rosier, when Juliette was so sick, Diane was constantly demanding that Juliette pick her up, and Juliette was constantly handing her off to Patrice. Juliette had only one month to live and said, She mustn't get used to me holding her, she'll miss it too much, afterward. Patrice now says that her first words were, Where is Mama? And the first film she loved was *Bambi*. She's watched the scene where Bambi understands his mother "can't be with him anymore" a hundred times; it's the closest she can come to her own story. Patrice also says that of the three girls Diane is the one who talks the most now about Juliette, and the only one who asks, often, to watch the slide show. The two of them go down to the basement and sit together in front of the computer screen. The music begins; the images appear. Patrice watches his wife. Diane watches her mother. Patrice watches Diane watch her mother. She cries, he cries, too, and there's a gentle comfort in crying together for the father and his little daughter, but he can't and won't ever again tell her what all fathers would always like to tell their children: Everything will be all right. And I who am so far away from them, who for the moment—and knowing how fragile this is—am happy, I would like to offer what solace I can, small comfort though it will be, and that's why this book is for Diane and her sisters.

My thanks to Colette Le Guay, Philippe Le Guay, and Belinda Cannone for our "work-and-play" visits to Montgoubert and for their friendship; thanks as well to Nicole, Pascale, and Hervé Clerc, for our time in Le Levron and for their friendship, too.

About the Author

EMMANUEL CARRÈRE, novelist, filmmaker, journalist, and biographer, is the award-winning internationally renowned author of *The Adversary* (a *New York Times* Notable Book), *My Life as a Russian Novel*, *Class Trip*, and *The Mustache*. Carrère lives in Paris.

About the Translator

LINDA COVERDALE has translated more than sixty books. A Chevalier de l'Ordre des Arts et des Lettres, she has won the International IMPAC Dublin Literary Award, the Scott Moncrieff Prize, and the French-American Foundation Translation Prize.